GUNS DOWN

GUNS DOWN

HOW TO DEFEAT THE NRA AND BUILD A SAFER FUTURE WITH FEWER GUNS

IGOR VOLSKY

THE NEW PRESS

NEW YORK
LONDON

Requests for permission to reproduce selections from this book should be mailed to: Permissions Department, The New Press, 120 Wall Street, 31st floor, New York, NY 10005.

Published in the United States by The New Press, New York, 2019
Distributed by Two Rivers Distribution

ISBN 978-1-62097-320-2 (ebook)

LIBRARY OF CONGRESS CATALOGING-IN-PUBLICATION DATA

Names: Volsky, Igor, 1986- author.
Title: Guns down : how to defeat the NRA and build a safer future with fewer guns / Igor Volsky.
Description: London : New York, 2019. | Includes bibliographical references and index.
Identifiers: LCCN 2018052117 | ISBN 9781620973196 (hc : alk. paper)
Subjects: LCSH: Gun control—United States. | Firearms ownership—United States. | Firearms and crime—United States. | Public safety—United States.
Classification: LCC HV7436 .V65 2019 | DDC 363.330973—dc23
LC record available at https://lccn.loc.gov/2018052117

The New Press publishes books that promote and enrich public discussion and understanding of the issues vital to our democracy and to a more equitable world. These books are made possible by the enthusiasm of our readers; the support of a committed group of donors, large and small; the collaboration of our many partners in the independent media and the not-for-profit sector; booksellers, who often hand-sell New Press books; librarians; and above all by our authors.

www.thenewpress.com

Book design and composition by Bookbright Media
This book was set in Janson Text and Avenir

Printed in the United States of America

10 9 8 7 6 5 4 3 2 1

CONTENTS

PREFACE: SHOOTING GUNS IN THE DESERT CAN SURPRISE YOU

"We do not teach people how to shoot; we teach them how to think," Mike, the second-in-command at one of the nation's largest firearms training institutes, tells me over an early dinner. We are at a country club twenty miles north of the gun range where I just spent the last two days firing two hundred rounds of ammunition and learning how to safely carry and operate a handgun.

A tall, distinguished-looking man who bears a slight resemblance to former president George H.W. Bush, Mike is wearing a yellow polo shirt, neat, clean khakis, and a belt with a holstered handgun and two full magazines. As we sit in front of a beautiful Rocky Mountain backdrop, the tops of which will be covered with snow in a matter of months, I take a big swig of coffee and search for a tactful way to ask Mike the question that has been swirling around my brain since my first day of training at the firearms institute.

I blurt out, "I still don't understand why you're lying to your clients." A silence falls over our table. As Mike looks away from me, I look directly at him and wait for him to respond.

Forty-eight hours earlier, I had boarded a plane to learn how to shoot a handgun from the best instructors in the business. The opportunity arose through my friend Sam (not his real name), who, in the course of my writing this book, has become my guide to the world of firearm enthusiasts. Sam invited me to travel to the Southwest and experience a two-day elite firearm training course with people he described as the best instructors in the world. "I will take it with you, and then after, you can interview all of the trainers," he said. "They all hate the NRA." He had arranged for the range to comp me the two-day course and rental equipment, plus complete access to the other students, instructors, and its leadership team.

Sam, a white, boyish, fast-talking ex-Marine and hardcore gun enthusiast, had passionately pitched the idea to me by phone months earlier: "You'll love it and really get a taste for what it's all about, meet some great people, and I'll do it with you." Fashioning myself an open-minded and adventurous person, I jumped at the chance. Surround myself with six hundred armed Americans and thousands of rounds of ammunition for two full days of gun shooting in a hot desert? Sign me up. What could go wrong?

So there I am, a city slicker who hasn't sat behind the wheel of a car in three or four years, driving my fully insured economy rental car literally into a desert at sunrise one Friday morning in October. I'm blasting a local hits station with the windows rolled down, singing at the top of my lungs in an effort to wake myself up enough to handle a handgun. Yes, I'm belting out Sia while doing seventy down a dirt road without another car in sight.

As I get closer, I turn off the radio, make the right turn, and take a deep, deep breath. Ahead of me, I see a line of cars about thirty deep and a large sign displaying the logo of the institute. Next to it is a larger placard:

WARNING

UNSAFE TO ENTER WITHOUT AUTHORIZATION

LIVE-FIRE TRAINING AREA

RISK OF SEVERE BODILY INJURY OR DEATH

I have arrived!

Before I know it, I'm on a five-hundred-acre compound in the middle of the mountains. I drive up to the parking lot, suddenly overcome by the vastness of this place, and pull into a spot.

Sam meets me and tells me that more than six hundred people will be taking twenty different classes at the institute that day, most of which involve handguns and rifles. After lunch, classes on automatic machine guns will be available.

My eyes grow wide at the idea of even being near a machine gun. I smile at him and look around to see people carrying coolers and equipment, behaving as if they're at an amusement park or some kind of sporting event. This is my first feeling of panic, of being found out as an interloper—or, worse, a spy—in a foreign world. We move into a line for equipment rentals, and Sam points out the people in the best tactical outfits and reviews their looks. Finally, something I can get into.

Sam himself is decked out in a slick black shirt, which accentuates his military build, and inverted cargo pants with pockets that expand into the leg, an outfit suited for concealed carry, he tells me. Everyone around us is wearing a variation of this military-style clothing, and I realize that these are specialty clothes designed for recreational firearms shooting. Some even have custom hats with their names embroidered on the front and back, as if they're actually serving in the military. These folks are really hardcore. "It has really become a lifestyle," Sam says to me.

I glance down at my jeans and bright red sneakers and realize I've made a horrible mistake. As if reading my mind, he says, "You're fine!" and starts to examine the "kit" the young attendant has just handed me, making sure I have everything I need.

We move forward toward a long row of tables where staffers are inspecting all weapons and ammunition. "It's his first time here,"

Sam says. "Magazines, two hundred rounds of ammunition, safety goggles, electronic ear protection, holsters . . . you got it all," the inspector says, mostly for my benefit. I smile and make a mental note that those things that hold the bullets are called "magazines," not "clips," and oh, by the way, it's "rounds," not "bullets."

"Okay, lift your hands up," the attendant says, and before I know it, he and Sam are putting a belt around my waist and sliding the ammunition holder and the gun holster onto it. The inspector confidently drops a Glock 17 into the gun holster on my right side—the firing side—and I'm carrying a firearm for the very first time in my life.

As Sam and I start to walk away, I try to decide if I feel any different. Suddenly, the inspector calls out after us. "Wait, are you *the* Sam?" he asks. Sam turns around and smiles.

"I've seen your videos and stuff," the inspector enthusiastically tells him, becoming a starstruck fan girl right before our eyes. "Thanks for everything you're doing to protect the Second Amendment," he adds, shaking Sam's hand. There it is, I think, the very first reference to the bitter political fight over this issue. It's always simmering just below the surface, isn't it?

We follow a mass of students into the building next to the inspection range. I gasp. The room is humongous, lined with tables from wall to wall, a raised platform with a podium in the front and two projectors. It seems to fit about four hundred people, and by the time we walk in they're almost all seated, with their hats on, looking at an instructor delivering welcoming remarks.

Everyone has an introductory packet that includes an itinerary and a form releasing the range from liability if the training results in "physical or emotional injury, paralysis, death, or damage to myself, to property, or to third parties." I sign the forms and comfort myself with the thought that holding the range liable for injury in the court of Twitter is still a viable option.

The speaker at the podium dutifully reviews every sentence in the liability form and gives us some basic safety guidelines. Sam, meanwhile, is decoding the gun-specific terms with whispers in my ear, and I nod along. I glance at the agenda. It is very full—and very precise. Almost every minute of our day is meticulously planned. This, if nothing else, puts me at ease.

Ten minutes later, Sam and I drive out to our assigned range. I see a mound of rock behind the man-shaped targets. The ground is composed of pebbles, though the area near the targets has lines of concrete to mark distances of three, five, and fifteen feet away from the target. This is where we will be shooting from, I reason.

Sam and I sit down in chairs next to each other. I look up and see four instructors—three men and one woman—standing in front of us. Sam hands me sunscreen, and it hits me that we're going to be outside in the desert heat all day long. I'm wearing a hat I've borrowed from the institute with my name written on two pieces of masking tape, on the front and back, a mandatory piece of clothing that will protect my face—from both the sun and other far more dangerous things. The hat will enable the coaches to yell at me if and when I do something wrong. I begin slathering the sun protection on my arms and face as the instructors introduce themselves and briefly tell us about their experiences with firearms, from military training to civilian instruction to law enforcement.

"This is a self-defense course. We will teach you how to defend yourself with a handgun, should the need ever arise," one of the mustached male instructors tells us. He is a jovial guy with a stocky build; he peppers his remarks with jokes as though he's doing some kind of gun stand-up comedy routine. The instruction on the range will be as scripted and smooth as the registration process, I suddenly realize. They sure know how to put a newbie at ease.

Our class of forty-four is about evenly split between first-time and returning students. Most are white middle-aged men, but about 20 percent are women. There are families with children as young as ten or twelve outfitted with the same gear that I'm now wearing—

and probably better shots. Seeing a Glock strapped to the waist of a twelve-year-old is a little like seeing a young boy put on his father's suit jacket: it's cute, but you don't want him walking out the door like that.

The stocky jovial instructor reviews the different parts of the firearm and its functionality. We are not allowed to touch the guns that are harnessed to our hips until we understand these basic fundamentals—e.g., never point the muzzle of the gun at anything you do not intend to shoot!—and we review some key processes using our "finger guns." We start with the fundamentals. Loading, unloading, aiming. The instruction is very even. Smooth. Methodical. It is clear that the coaches are operating from a memorized script, and I assume that if I were to walk over to the range next door, its group of instructors would be saying the very same thing at the very same time.

Once everyone is comfortable, we walk out to the three-foot line on the range and are told that for the next two days we will be divided into two rallies and partnered with a student coach who will help us move through the instruction and correct any basic mistakes we make.

Sam and I decide that we want to shoot at the same time, so I pair with Tim, a fifty-something Asian man who has taken the course before and is staying at the institute for two additional days to study rifle shooting. I sheepishly explain to him that this is my first time shooting a gun and that I hope he has a lot of patience. He smiles at me kindly and promises to help instruct me.

I'm learning how to take the firearm out of the holster and put it back in, and how to load and unload ammunition. Before I know it, I am standing fifteen yards in front of the target, wearing eye protection and electronic ear protection, about to fire my very first round. Tim is standing behind my right shoulder, walking me through all of the steps I have to go through to make sure my firearm is safe enough to shoot.

Chamber check, magazine check, insert magazine, run the slide, chamber check, magazine check, aim, let the slack out, push.

Finally I push the trigger, and hit my target somewhere below the waist. An instructor comes over to me—another mustached man who served in Vietnam—and reminds me of the proper way to pull a trigger in order to exert maximum trigger control. He tells me I'm pushing the trigger too hard in anticipation of the shot and aiming too low as a result. I have to first take the slack out of the trigger, then continue applying pressure until the firearm goes off. The surprise of the moment will prevent me from inadvertently shifting my aim in anticipation of the shot. The instructor asks me to take several more shots, but I struggle to place the steps in sequence and my rounds land all over my target.

"Dude, you just shot a gun, from the holster! Did you ever think you'd do that?" Sam asks me.

I'm not sure. I am feeling somewhat exhilarated by the experience, but I have no great desire to do it again. I'm also tired and hungry and definitely overwhelmed. This is far more complicated than I imagined. Shooting here is a series of choreographed maneuvers. Trying to do all the steps right and in sequence is a mental struggle. I'm overwhelmed by the sheer number of things I need to remember.

Chamber check, magazine check, insert magazine, run the slide, chamber check, magazine check, aim, let the slack out, push.

As we break for lunch—exactly at 12:30 as the agenda predicted—Sam leans over to me and says that I have already completed more firearm instruction than most states require for a concealed-carry permit. I feel stunned. I would never trust myself to use a gun in a stressful real-life situation, yet millions of Americans who own weapons have less knowledge about how to properly fire and use a firearm than I do! The thought of this scares me, and I turn to the only thing that will comfort me in this moment: a chicken nugget sandwich with fries from the food truck parked on the property.

Over lunch, an instructor named Bridget gives us a presentation on "firearms in the real world." I nod along, and then something Bridget says startles me.

"Sooner or later, we are all asking to be targeted, asking to be picked off," she says. The people around me, those who are listening, do not seem alarmed and I look up at the PowerPoint slides that are guiding the lecture to find a color-coded alert system.

- Condition white: you are an easy target.
- Condition yellow: you are alert, less likely to be targeted.
- Condition orange: you know in advance what you are going to do when danger comes.
- Condition red: you are facing a specific threat and know exactly how to take it out.
- Condition black: the bad guy has crossed a line and you are going to take him out.

"You want to spend most of your life in condition yellow," Bridget says, "and remember to develop your combat mind-set." She urges us to explain this to our friends and co-workers, to educate them about the criminals and murderers who are roaming our streets, hiding behind every bush and building, ready to jump out and threaten us. "We all know what the world is like today. All you have to do is turn on the news. The more of us who're paying attention, the safer our world will be, the safer our communities will be."

I fight to suppress a jolt of anger. I had come here because Sam and Mike had assured me of its unique place in gun culture. Mike had described it in an early email arranging the trip as a facility that is "an intelligent option between the far right and far left logic on this topic."

But here was an instructor telling six hundred mostly white, middle-aged attendees who'd just spent the morning shooting handguns and rifles to always carry their firearms, to remain constantly alert to danger. The instructor is telling them that this danger is not just a probability we face by living in the modern world; it is an absolute inevitability. To make matters worse, the lecture is being delivered a little more than two weeks before the 2016 presidential election, and I immediately recognize the echo of Donald Trump's stump speeches, in which he warns Americans of an invisible wave of crime, even though homicides continue to be at historic lows—especially for white people, who are far less likely to be victims of gun violence than black people.

Sitting there, you would think that an assailant could break into the classroom at any moment. It's a miracle that these Americans were even able to live this long, to outsmart the criminals and crime plaguing their communities and make it to this critical life-affirming training alive!

I express these misgivings to Sam, and he agrees that some of the language does sound a bit alarmist and encourages me to bring it up with Mike over our scheduled dinner the following day. I vow to do so and we return to the range. But this time, something feels different. I am no longer viewing this experience as just hundreds of gun nerds engaging in a recreational activity of their choice and doing so safely and responsibly. I see people who have driven out to the desert to take a two- or four-day course and spend hundreds or thousands of dollars learning how to protect themselves from the bogeyman. As I sit back down, I spot several NRA shirts I had missed before. A couple of people are wearing Trump/Pence shirts that I had clocked but dismissed as expected representations of the political climate. Now they've suddenly taken on new, more sinister meaning. These are not just gun enthusiasts. These are people whose gun ownership identifies them with a divisive conservative political ideology and identity that prides itself on "trolling" or "owning" libs.

The woman sitting in front of us tells us she carries her weapon absolutely everywhere she goes, to protect her family. She coordinates her gun and holster with her clothes and can't imagine leaving home without either. She adds that her children would constantly bump into her firearm when they were younger, but now they know how to avoid brushing up against it during hugs.

That afternoon, as we're getting up to shoot, I'm growing more and more frustrated by a feeling of isolation. It's as if I've fallen into some crazy conservative conspiracy Facebook feed. I'm still overwhelmed by the complexity of technically shooting a gun the right way. Who can remember all of these steps in an actual gunfight?

Chamber check, magazine check, insert magazine, run the slide, chamber check, magazine check, aim, let the slack out, push.

I'm counting down the hours and then the minutes, telling Sam I think I need to just go to my Airbnb and rest afterward. He suggests/insists that I attend the special concealed-carry lecture that ends the day, and I just sigh. "It will really get to the morality of using our firearms," he reminds me, "and will probably break though some of the paranoia we heard earlier." I realize he's right. I have to suck it up. I've flown all the way into the desert to experience a real gun course; I should take full advantage of it.

After I leave my rented weapon with the range instructor, we make our way back to the lecture hall for the concealed-carry lecture. The instructor who had thanked Sam that morning for protecting the Second Amendment spots us and comes over to talk. He's a tall, skinny man with dirty blond hair and a friendly manner. The words LINE INSTRUCTOR are printed on his T-shirt. Sam informs him that I have just shot my first firearm and he looks at me approvingly, mentioning how much he enjoys working here. Sam prods him as to why—more for my benefit than his own, I suspect—and he pauses, looks at both of us, and says, "In case the foreigners invade from China or Hillary turns tyrannical or there's a mass shooting." Sam and I fall silent, staring at him. He adds, "I just want to be ready for the worst."

"Oh, you cannot believe that conspiracy shit," Sam says with a laugh, glancing over at me nervously. "You just cannot believe that," he repeats, now jovially slapping the line instructor on the back and chuckling, trying to laugh the whole thing off.

The two of them change the subject and are now discussing some kind of specialty pants that the range has switched to per Sam's suggestion. They talk some more about gear, and I glance at my watch, suddenly growing impatient. I have an urge to get away from the line instructor and into the classroom. Sam has been good about not outing me, not telling people that I'm on book research, but I worry that the line instructor will ask me where I live, what I do, why I'm here. I've thought of some stock replies I could offer if asked, but like the handgun I'm still not sure how to operate, I don't actually want to deploy them.

We finally break away from the line instructor, and I just shoot Sam a look. We're walking into the large classroom with the long tables and the four hundred people and I see Bridget back at the podium. She's using a PowerPoint slide show, and I spot two projections on each side of the room with information about the consequences of actually shooting your firearm. I'm reminded again how massive this whole operation is, and I grow a little depressed. People have traveled from all over the country to be told that they need to be afraid of being killed on a daily basis. On the screen, Bridget is helping us identify what our enemy could look like.

"There are some obvious examples," she says, and a picture of a Latino gang member comes on screen. "But who else?" she asks. "Hillary Clinton!" someone yells out from the crowd, and the room breaks out in hearty laughter.

"All right, all right," Bridget says with a chuckle, moving her hands outward and then pushing them down in a gesture designed to calm down the crowd. Sam and I look at each other, and I slump even lower in my chair. "A gunfight is risky business. You risk everything and win absolutely nothing," Bridget repeats several times. It's a theme in the speech, and I recognize that the institute is clearly hoping to impart a message of restraint—but it's not breaking through the context of paranoia surrounding the lecture.

- "There is no such thing as an unarmed man."
- "Do not think you can't use deadly force if they don't have a weapon."
- "We shouldn't let people get too close to us so people don't have an opportunity to harm us."
- "Next time you're sitting with your family or in a grocery store line, think of what you would do if a person had a gun. Try to create different scenarios so you're preparing your brain to kick in and act almost like muscle memory."
- "It doesn't take much to know what the world is like. All you have to do is watch the news and you'll be shaking in your boots. It's a different world now. Stay in condition yellow."

At one point, she suggests that one way to protect yourself from unfair prosecution if you end up in court after a gunfight is to write a letter to yourself detailing how you have trained to defuse and stop aggressive situations in order to protect your family. "Send the letter to yourself via certified letter. Sign for it, but do not open it," Bridget instructs. "If you have to use deadly force, that letter could be used to let the jury know why you did what you did. It will make your actions seem more reasonable," Bridget says, placing an extra emphasis on the word *reasonable*.

The lecture ends, and Sam and I go our separate ways. I drive back to my Airbnb and reflect on the forces behind this place—a business model that I am realizing is at least in part based on scaring people into coming back time and time again. I thought I was entering a space of gun enthusiasts living out their "martial values," as Sam had put it to me during our initial conversations. While there certainly is a militia aspect to the training and attitude of my fellow classmates, the training is intertwined with political and social anxieties.

As I go to bed that night, I make a list of questions to ask Mike at our dinner the following day. At the very top is this one: why are you pandering to students who believe their Second Amendment rights are seconds from being infringed, reinforcing their sense of victimhood and fear, then sending them out into the world armed and paranoid?

On day two, we do not need to meet at the range until 7:45 in the morning. I wake up with plenty of time to take a shower and get dressed, but as I look into my travel bag to pull out a fresh T-shirt, I freeze. Among the pairs of socks and underwear, I find just two shirts. One dark blue Georgetown Law School T-shirt and a gray one with the words CENTER FOR AMERICAN PROGRESS on the back.

Thought one: *I really need to learn to pack the night before rather than the morning of.*

Thought two: *What the fuck am I going to wear today?*

I cannot put on the Georgetown shirt without eliciting suspicion or even ridicule from my classmates. The Center for American Progress shirt is also a no-go. I can't get away with wearing the logo of a group associated with the woman they joked about murdering less than twenty-four hours ago. A quick Google search reveals that the closest Target or Walmart is more than forty miles away, so I grudgingly put on the same green shirt from day one.

Back on the range that morning, we're learning how to clear the different jams that could come up in the midst of a gunfight, and I struggle mightily. I find the steps difficult to remember and the process of

setting up the jam cumbersome. We have to go through ten or twelve
different steps in quick succession, and at one point I fall behind. One
of the instructors is standing several yards behind us with a bullhorn,
repeating the choreographed procession of instructions.

Chamber check, magazine check, insert magazine, run the slide, cham-
ber check, magazine check, aim, let the slack out, push.

I try to rush through to keep up and accidentally pull the trigger.
Thankfully, the gun is unloaded and nothing happens. But I immediately feel I need to stop. We sit back down and I start trying to
think of a way to get out of the class without offending or jeopardiz-
ing my dinner with Mike. Luckily, it's time for lunch; Sam and I go
back to the classroom to eat. It's another lecture about how to avoid
being detained in the aftermath of a gunfight. Bridget is back up
there offering sample answers we need to give to the police to avoid
being arrested or serving jail time—answers that would sound good
to a jury, should it come to that.

After lunch we get back to our range and a truck with bleach-
er seats in its bed is waiting to take us to a house simulation. The
instructors announce that the exercise will test our ability to defend
our homes from intruders, and we load up. I'm nervous about having
to shoot a gun outside of the range, in a more realistic environment,
but I climb onto the truck and hope for the best. Beside me is an
older, heavier gentleman, who I learn has made the trek to the desert from Connecticut. He bemoans the state's tight gun restrictions
and says, "If this election goes the wrong way, we'll all be living in
FEMA camps without any ability to defend ourselves." I start to say
something, but then stop, not sure how to reply to something like
that. Do I agree? Do I try to challenge his logic? I decide to leave it
alone and look away toward the mountains, pretend I am mesmerized by the scenery. We arrive at the simulation point and I see two
hastily constructed houses. We each take turns going in with an
instructor, who walks us through the process of shooting pictures of

intruders who pop up from behind the windows. The experience is far less stressful than I expected. I shoot at pictures of humans who look threatening and pop out at me from different areas of the house. There is a certain concentrated rhythm to this exercise, and I begin to enjoy it.

On our walk back to the range Sam is pumped, and he asks me what I think of this "Disneyland of guns." I chuckle and realize that this is exactly how the institute is presenting itself. It is also quickly expanding, building new, more complex ranges, and developing a resort component that will allow vacationers to buy time-shares and stay out in the desert shooting guns for weeks at a time.

We get back to our range and spend the afternoon just firing off rounds. I finally realize that the trick to aiming is to focus on the front sight of your weapon while allowing the target to become blurry. My instructors and my partner, Tim, have reminded me of this almost every time I pulled the trigger, but it took a while for my brain to actually process the information.

At the end of the day, I return my rented equipment—feeling lighter almost instantly!—and speed off to meet Mike at the country club down the road.

Mike gives me a warm handshake and sits down next to me. He comments briefly on the beauty of our surroundings and launches right into his pitch. He sees the training facility as the political middle ground between crazy right-wing gun enthusiasts and gun control advocates. He hopes its emphasis on increasing training standards could be supported by people on all sides of the debate.

Mike is also laying it on thick. He has Googled me enough to learn that I was the LGBT content editor at *ThinkProgress*. He informs me that the institute employs a transgender person and that gay people often come to the range. (It's sweet—the kind of thing a straight person thinks a gay person wants to hear.) The training institute, he stresses, strives for diversity and has a high number of women who take its courses and a good number of African Americans. I listen to him and decide that the best way to address my concerns about the institute is to ask him about them directly.

"I really enjoyed my time on the range," I begin. "The staff was incredibly professional and knowledgeable, and the instruction was top-notch. But I was very disappointed in your lectures."

That's when I blurt out my tactless question.

After an uncomfortable moment, I say, "It's one thing to tell students, 'I have a Second Amendment right to own and use a firearm, and if I'm going to do that, then I'm going to come here and get the best training I can to exercise that right.' This is what you're describing to me as the mission of the school. But it's another thing to tell students that there's a criminal on every street corner and that gun violence is almost inevitable."

"Those statements are irresponsible and not our doctrine," Mike quickly assures me. He concedes that some instructors do go off script during lectures but tells me he is in the process of videotaping those presentations in order to avoid the kind of fear mentality that I experienced.

"I guess what I can't understand is why you're telling your students that violence is on the rise and their lives are in danger, if that is not empirically true." While there are large geographic variations in crime rates, overall the violent crime rate fell by 48 percent from 1993 to 2016.[1]

Mike looks away and then down to the table, as if I have disappointed him. "The increase in peripheral awareness—head on a swivel, keep aware of your surroundings—is probably the number-one thing you can do to live a long and healthy life, irrespective of the communities in which you live or travel.

"The skill set of color-coded awareness is just a habit, like brushing and flossing your teeth. I don't consider it paranoia," he says. "I will sit in a place where I'll have multiple choices for exiting, where

I can see someone who is a problem coming in. You can go through your life and never have a problem, but tomorrow's paper will show someone who didn't think they were going to have a problem tonight either. It's a matter of preparedness. I don't live my life frisking people, but I don't know that you can depend on law enforcement as a solver of problems in all cases. In many cases where seconds count, the police are minutes away."

I look at him incredulously and say, "But your lectures aren't just telling people to be vigilant. They're instructing them that crime is inevitable. When you drop those kinds of statements into the conspiracy theories and paranoia that are prevalent throughout our culture and you add guns to the mix, you're asking for violence."

"My answer is, our lectures . . . when we were smaller and had one guy doing the lectures, they were memorized and it was scripted word for word. We now have maybe a dozen staff that provide lectures, and quite candidly it's not as tight as our on-range content, and what I started, and we're doing it right now, is a video project where we'll have someone do all of the lectures, we'll script it in advance and update it so it's not going to have unreasonable fear-and-threat crap in it."

"So, the new lectures are not going to be instigating fear?" I ask, to clarify.

"When I get through the new script that we'll draft and sign off on, it'll be 'The world can be a very dangerous place and problems can go from a walk in the park to danger, but it all depends on where you are and where you live.' I do not like fearmongering," he says, then adds, "We also may be overstating for dramatic effect and to make sure that you're paying attention, but I totally object to the Chinese hordes or that Hillary Clinton will take away their guns."

I take Mike at his word. He seems far from the type who spends his nights on alt-right websites. But I also suspect that he uses the fearmongering as a business opportunity: meeting his clients where they are, serving and catering to their beliefs and prejudices just as the NRA manipulates fears of a gun grab to drive up gun sales. He's certainly not going to any great lengths to dispute such myths.

I turn to the question of policy. "Ideally, in my perfect world, all Americans would have to obtain a license before they can buy and operate a gun, proving that they know how to use the firearm, and then renew it every so often, undergoing a background check each time."

To my surprise, Mike agrees. "If you were to wave a magic wand and make that happen, I would personally agree with you, because that's the business that we are in, but I would add to that that it should be a federal standard and it should be 'shall issue' instead of 'may issue.'" He adds that he wants the government to deal with this once and for all, in a big compromise that doesn't create a slippery slope that could lead to even more restrictions.

"My concern is that the end game of the most severe liberal is the elimination of the individual's right to possess a weapon for self-defense. The equally idiotic right-wing position is that regardless of your psychological soundness and skill level, you should be able to have not only small arms but also rockets and put them in a backpack and carry them to school. Those are not going to happen—either one of them—so rational folks like yourself should be able to come to a compromise. Just arm-wrestle it one damn time and be done with it," he recommends.

Mike goes on to argue that carrying a weapon in public should be even more restricted: you should need a "graduate-level skill set" from a four-day handgun class to be allowed to conceal and carry in public. He admits that that description would apply to only a tiny percentage of those who come through his institute, and an even smaller portion of those who currently own guns overall.

"I used to live in Southern California and had a concealed-carry permit that I had to renew every two years," he says. "I would go to a range in order to take the skills test. Almost everyone else there was a retired cop or a private eye. The test basically was, do not shoot yourself in the foot, and the target was the size of Schwarzenegger from three yards. It was embarrassingly nonexistent in skill and they could barely pass it. None of them should have a concealed-carry permit. It's just that simple."

As our dinner comes to a close, I thank Mike for his time and generosity.

For all the discomfort I felt at his range, his openness to having a rational conversation about increasing standards and support for federal gun licensing left me hopeful. It made me feel that if we organize our communities and he organizes his, maybe we'll be able to fix this thing after all.

GUNS DOWN

INTRODUCTION: WHY YOU SHOULD GIVE UP YOUR GUNS

When people ask me, "Are you really trying to take people's guns away?" I respond, "Yes, I am."

I want to decrease the number of guns in circulation and make guns harder to get. This is the only way we will reduce firearm suicides and gun violence in America and save the lives of more than 38,000 men, women, and children who fall victim to bullets every single year.

It is that simple.

While I want to be honest about my intentions up front, I also want you to hear me out, no matter your thoughts on the gun debate. *Guns Down* makes an evidence-based argument about the importance of reducing the number of guns in the United States. The argument is bold. It is radical. It is a departure from the usual rhetoric of gun-control advocates. It is a plan that would have been embraced by our founding fathers. It is a plan that will actually work.

For far too long, gun control advocates have focused too much on telling people what we think they want to hear or what we believe is politically feasible in the moment. We worry that being up-front or honest with our intentions will alienate the public or play into the claims of gun control opponents who regularly accuse us of acting like gun grabbers. And so we let ourselves be snookered by the fake patriotism of the gun lobby. We allow that lobby to wrap its rhetoric in the American flag and obscure the horrific consequences of its deadly agenda. We give its arguments the same weight as the opinions—and lives—of the overwhelming majority of Americans. We accept the myth of the superpatriotic gun owner and even perpetuate it.

I cringe any time gun control proponents preface conversations or debates about gun safety with how much they respect gun owners and the Second Amendment.

The traditional gun control argument goes something like this: "I don't want to take away anybody's guns; I believe in the Second Amendment. I think we should pass commonsense reforms like universal background checks that keep guns out of the hands of the *wrong* people."

We have heard this argument since the shooting at Columbine High School on April 20, 1999. Two decades since that tragedy devastated the nation and opened our collective eyes to the dangers of weak gun laws, we have gone out of our way to talk about the Second Amendment. During that period, we have failed to pass even modest reforms that would make it harder for people to obtain firearms or reduce the deadly consequences of gun violence—and the gun industry and its allies still use fears of mass gun confiscation to oppose any and all changes.

Meanwhile, we now have more guns in the United States than people. Americans make up 5 percent of the world population, but own nearly half of the civilian-owned guns in the world. Is it any wonder, then, that more Americans have died from guns in the last fifty years than in all of the wars in American history? Or that more Americans have died or been injured in school shootings than in the entire previous century?[1] We are 10 times more likely to be killed by guns than citizens of other high-income nations; 56 percent more likely to die from a gunshot than in a traffic accident; 11 times more likely to be assaulted with a gun than to be harmed by a hurricane, lightning strike, flood, or another force of nature; and 128 times more likely to die in a domestic gun assault than in an international terrorist incident!

Those statistics are just the beginning. Gun violence plagues many of our cities and is reflected in the police violence perpetrated against our young African American men. It could claim any of us at any time, but it claims the marginalized most often.

The truth is, the gun lobby has no interest in protecting our constitutional rights. No, the National Rifle Association (NRA)—the popular face of the gun industry—is focused on helping gun manufacturers sell more guns; more gun sales mean more money for the lobby and more foot soldiers for its political battles. The lobby stakes out bold, extreme positions to advance its guns-everywhere-and-for-everyone agenda and it doesn't give an inch.

The tepid strategy gun control advocates have pursued over the last several decades, on the other hand, appeals to risk-averse politicians and political consultants worried about alienating certain voters. It forces gun control advocates to start the debate by accepting falsehoods propagated by the gun industry—namely that we can reduce gun violence by simply concentrating all of the firearms in the hands of so-called responsible gun owners—and pushes them to argue against themselves. This weak strategy also dismisses the fact that an overwhelming majority of Americans are on our side. They want to build a future with fewer guns; they're just waiting for political leaders to channel this widespread public support for gun safety policies into a popular movement that could bring about real change. This much is clear: our fear of asking for what we really want has allowed the gun lobby to contort a debate about a basic human need—safety—into a conversation about the meaning of patriotism and the Second Amendment.

It is time to assert our right to *safety* and to actively fight for that right without apology.

Safety from gun violence is a basic human need, and we must

design and implement a plan to achieve it. Parents should not have to worry about whether their children will come home from school, cities should not be besieged by gun violence, we should not have to mentally design an exit plan from crowded sports stadiums or concerts just in case, nor should we fear opening our social media feeds and being confronted by another mass shooting, or by a domestic dispute or robbery attempt turned deadly. Such fear is not a normal characteristic of a representative democracy that prides itself on building a government "of the people, by the people, for the people." It is characteristic of a democracy hijacked by special interests that have spent millions of dollars polluting our public discourse, buying off our politicians, and re-orienting our government toward increasing their profits rather than promoting the general welfare of the people.

It's time to admit that a policy of trying to make sure that only "responsible people" have guns is just not working. It's not protecting our citizens. It's not resonating with the public. And it's not pushing Americans to prioritize gun control in the voting booth.

This book takes an entirely different approach to the issue of guns in the United States. Rather than tinkering with changes on the edges, like expanding background checks and closing loopholes in existing laws, *Guns Down* envisions a bold long-term goal: a country where guns are scarce and can be purchased only by individuals who have proven themselves to be responsible. I do not advocate for banning all firearms, however. I believe that Americans should have the liberty to use firearms for hunting, sport, and self-protection. However, as the playwright George Bernard Shaw put it, "liberty means responsibility." And over the last several decades, the country has adopted laws that allow almost anyone to easily obtain a firearm and carry it outside the home—regardless of whether they know how to use their guns. We now must correct that imbalance by dramati-

cally increasing the standards for firearm ownership and reducing the number of firearms floating throughout our communities.

This book will also show how reduction of gun ownership has lowered gun violence throughout the world wherever it has been tried, and how it will lower the number of gun deaths in the United States. I'll unveil a bold set of policies called the New Second Amendment Compact that will achieve this vision and argue that most Americans support such reforms. I'll show how making guns significantly harder to get is fully consistent with the intentions of our founding fathers. I will lay out how we can build a popular movement that can drive support for these ideas and make them a reality.

But before we get started, I want to add a note of caution. A movement calling for gun reduction must be as diverse as America itself and prioritize solutions that do not repeat the mistakes of the past, such as criminalizing gun owners and sending them into a justice system where people of color are treated one way and white people are treated another. This movement must focus its solutions at the top of the gun distribution chain: gun manufacturers, dealers, and the lobby that gives them the political cover to operate with minimal regulation. It must advocate reforms that will invest in the communities most impacted by gun violence while also significantly increasing the standards for gun ownership by tightly regulating the sale and transfer of guns and ensuring that only individuals with proper training and knowledge can possess and purchase firearms.

We will not succeed in this goal next week, next month, or even next year. The great social movements of the past have taught us that big changes take time. Societal transformation requires effort, dedication, and the perseverance of Americans engaging in the democratic process: marching, shaming those in power, making them uncomfortable by holding them accountable, and voting—yes, voting!—for real change.

A colleague once told me that in politics, you do not get half a loaf of bread by asking for half a loaf. To build your movement and truly succeed, you must demand the full loaf. You have to shape and organize public opinion, not simply follow it.

It's Far Too Easy to Buy a Gun

Alex is a gun enthusiast who likes to go to the shooting range. He is very suspicious of gun control efforts and voted against a Nevada ballot measure to expand background check requirements to cover private firearm sales in the state. When my friend Allan and I asked him to purchase a gun from a private dealer, as part of our attempts to show just how easy it is to buy a gun in America, Alex agreed. But he felt sure that our experiment with him would fail. Surely no responsible gun owner would sell him a weapon online without putting him through a background check first!

The idea for this project originated in January 2018, when I part nered with NowThis, a popular digital news service, to go out to Las Vegas and visit the Shooting, Hunting, Outdoor Trade (SHOT) Show, the gun industry's largest trade show. The event was taking place just three months after and a little over a mile away from the largest individual mass murder in modern American history. The October 1, 2017, shooting at the Route 91 Harvest music festival left 58 people dead and 851 injured. SHOT Show wouldn't provide NowThis with press credentials to officially cover the event, but we were spending three days in Las Vegas anyway. We wanted to see if it was easier to obtain a firearm in Nevada than talk to the people at SHOT Show.

Allan and I logged on to Armslist and saw it all: handguns, assault weapons, bump stocks, etc. We just needed a Nevada resident to execute the purchase. (Federal guidelines prohibit a seller from transferring a gun to someone with an out-of-state license.) Luckily, Alex, a member of our crew, was in the market for a handgun and agreed to participate in our story.

Alex's love for guns is rooted in tragedy. His mother was gunned down when he was younger, and he believes that, had she had a gun to protect herself, she would still be with him today.

It took Alex just a couple of minutes to find a revolver he liked, and moments later the seller responded to his query. I remember telling Allan, "Wow! It would've taken longer for me to leave the hotel room where we are filming, get in line at Starbucks, and bring us back coffees than it did to set up that gun sale." We had spent ten minutes searching for a gun online and another five minutes waiting for our private seller to respond. In fifteen minutes, Alex was ready to drive out and pick up the firearm. As he took off with another member of our crew, Allan and I waited in our hotel room nervously.

We wondered if our experiment would work. Would a private seller *really* agree to sell an instrument designed to kill to another—no questions asked?

Less than three hours after we first started looking for a gun to buy, Alex walked back into our room with a revolver wrapped inside a little black bag that resembled a sock. He told us it took him less than five minutes to meet with the seller (an elderly man who seemed to be unloading his stockpile of weapons), hand over the money, take the gun, and get back into the car. The seller did not check any criminal database for Alex's name and did not ask him why he needed the gun or whether he knew how to use it. He didn't even try to find out if Alex's ID was authentic.

"He did do a bill of sale with his information," Alex said. "He had a copy that I put my information down, but that is it. I could have had a fake ID and put whatever I wanted down here and I could have walked away with a gun." He added rather grimly, "I'll be honest with you—it does not really sit well with me."

"At the very least, make it a little bit more difficult for someone to get their hands on a firearm," Alex told me. "It is pretty eye-opening. I'm pretty embarrassed with myself that I voted the other way, because this needs to be changed. You should not be able to get a gun that easily."

The United States suffers from a high number of mass shootings, everyday gun violence, and suicides because we have too many guns and they are too easy to get. In many states, it's easier to get a gun than to buy a beer. The United States allows practically anyone to acquire a firearm. People do not need a license to purchase one, and they don't need to show that they know how to use it. They just need to pony up the dollars.

Under our current laws, practically anybody can get a gun this way in many states throughout America. Are you a murderer? No problem, you can buy a gun from an unlicensed private seller. Did time for armed robbery? That's okay! Hit up another bank with a weapon you purchase online. Have a temporary restraining order for stalking your partner? You don't even have to go online for a gun; federal law is so weak, you can pass a background check! Convicted of threatening a mosque or a synagogue? No worries! The background-check system will clear you, too! Federal law prohibits convicted felons, domestic abusers, and people with histories of involuntary mental health treatment from passing a background check and buying a weapon from a federally licensed dealer, but you can almost always get around these prohibitions by buying from a private seller.

Most gun sellers are responsible, but many are no angels.[1] An undercover investigation in New York City found that 62 percent of private online firearm sellers made a sale even *after* a buyer disclosed that she or he could not pass a background check! The man who sold Alex his firearm did not know if Alex was a convicted criminal or another prohibited person. He chose not to ask, and, under our current broken system, he was under no obligation to do so. In a country where guns are ridiculously easy to get, gun deaths, as we shall see in the chapters ahead, are all too common.

Guns Kill Young People

A couple of years ago, researchers collected data on school violence around the world, studying every incident in which someone in a school was killed or a murder was attempted. They discovered fifty-seven incidents in thirty-six countries between 2000 and 2010. Nearly half of those incidents—twenty-eight—occurred in the United States. The United States had more incidents of school violence with a gun than Argentina, Australia, Azerbaijan, Belgium, Bosnia-Herzegovina, Brazil, Bulgaria, Canada, China, Denmark, England, Finland, France, Germany, Greece, Guatemala, Hungary, India, Israel, Italy, Japan, Kenya, Latvia, the Netherlands, Northern Ireland, Norway, Poland, Russia, Scotland, South Africa, South Korea, Swaziland, Thailand, Trinidad and Tobago, and Yemen—*combined*.

That alone should blow our minds. In fact, American teenagers are eighty-two times more likely to die from a gun homicide than their international peers. As the number of young people killed in car accidents has declined in recent decades, the number of young people killed by guns has risen. Youth gun violence has now overtaken motor vehicle accidents as a leading cause of death for young people in the United States, second only to drug overdose.[1] American students, in other words, are living on the front lines of our nation's gun problem; they deal with the consequences of weak laws every single day.

Just consider school lockdown drills—emergency exercises that have become as ubiquitous as chalkboards or lockers.

When I attended the March for Our Lives in Washington, DC, in March 2018, I asked students how it feels to undergo lockdown. What goes through their heads? How do they cope?

Children as young as seven years old told me about how they snuck over to one corner of the room and hid. Their teachers claimed they were preparing for a potential bear or some other animal entering the classroom.

Older students knew all too well for what they were training. Their reactions fell into two camps. Some described the fear and anguish they felt: the paranoia of not knowing whether the drill was real, the hope that they would never have to implement the skills they were learning. "Sadness pervades you for the rest of the day," one student told me. "You just have to compartmentalize it and move on with your life."

For others, the drills have become so routine, they no longer take them seriously. This feeling is best captured in the movie *Eighth Grade*, Bo Burnham's uncomfortably realistic portrayal of middle school life in 2017. Thirteen-year-old Kayla, the main character, crawls over to her male love interest during a shooter drill, breaking protocol. In the dark, the two engage in a sarcastic conversation about overpowering a potential shooter. The rest of the students are too consumed by their phones to care or notice and once the lights come back on, and Kayla is not under her desk, the classroom teacher displays mild annoyance, but no real alarm. The drill is now just another mundane fact of school life.

Lauren Hogg, a survivor of the school shooting in Parkland, Florida, described a similar nonchalant attitude toward lockdown drills in *#NeverAgain: A New Generation Draws the Line*, a book that she co-wrote with her brother, David, about the March for Our Lives movement. Hogg described how her schoolmates reacted when Marjory Stoneman Douglas High School went into lockdown as the shooting, which ultimately took seventeen lives, was unfolding.

"I was trying to run up the stairs as fast as I could, but all these juniors and seniors were like, 'Stop running, guys, it's fine,'" she writes. "When I was finally almost back to that classroom, I saw the librarians standing in the hallway, and all of a sudden their walkie-talkies were going off and they were listening to something, and then I just saw their faces go pale, and one librarian started screaming, 'Code red! Code red! Everybody get back to your classrooms now!' . . . And kids still thought it was a joke. They were laughing. That was how routine these drills had become. Or maybe it was more that the mind doesn't want to believe what it doesn't want to believe."[2]

Laughter may indeed serve as a coping mechanism during moments of crisis. A staggering 57 percent of teens say they fear a school shooting, and since the mass murder at Columbine High School in April of 1999, over 215,000 students have experienced gun violence in some form at school.[3]

I am thirty-three years old. When I was in school, I never once worried about a school shooting nor did I ever undergo a mass-shooting drill. If you are twenty or younger, you have. The number of public schools that run active-shooter drills keeps climbing with each high-profile school shooting. Why? Because rather than making it more difficult for students to obtain firearms in the first place, we're burdening students and school districts with the responsibility of avoiding the bullets once they leave the barrel of the gun.

In the 2003–2004 school year, the year I graduated from high school, fewer than 50 percent of public schools had some form of active-shooter drill. That number grew to 70 percent in December 2013, the year after the shooting at Sandy Hook Elementary School.

It hovers somewhere around 95 percent today, according to the National Center for Education Statistics.[4] Most students undergo one of two types of drills: a "code yellow" lockdown, wherein a teacher simply locks the door but otherwise keeps teaching uninterrupted, and a "code red" lockdown, in which teachers must do precisely what many did during the horrific school shootings in Parkland and Newtown—usher students away from windows and doors, turn off lights, and stay silent.[5]

In six states, students undergo more specific active-shooter drills based on the worst case scenario: a gunman with explicit intentions to murder. Often these drills involve local law enforcement and real guns.[6] In some cases, police departments and school districts hire companies that bring in props, including fake blood and men in masks with plastic guns, to make sure everyone is prepared. This is a real-life mass-shooting role-play scenario we are designing for our children. To be an American student is to undergo an active-shooter lockdown drill, a concept entirely foreign to our Japanese, Canadian, British, or Australian counterparts.

Yet as horrific and traumatic as these drills can be, they do give me hope. The lockdown drills students undergo today are reminiscent of the duck-and-cover exercises that students of the 1950s and early 1960s performed in case the Soviet Union were to launch its handful of nuclear bombs against the United States. At the time, we believed that an attack could destroy major American cities but that rural areas of the country could potentially survive, particularly if Americans had some degree of training. Seven decades later, we are relying on similar drills to protect our youth from a *domestic* threat that we ourselves have created, not the actions of a foreign adversary whose behavior we cannot control. But if the duck-and-cover exercises of the Cold War era transformed students into antinuclear activists and inspired many to lead the social equality movements that dominated the 1960s, 1970s, and 1980s, including the civil rights movement, women's liberation, and the push for LGBT equality, then students' experiences with active-shooter drills today may be pushing an entire generation of advocates to fight for stricter gun controls.

In the aftermath of the Parkland shooting, young people took to the streets to advocate for gun safety and launched massive campaigns to register their peers to vote. They're channeling their first-hand experiences with America's broken gun laws into action that is forcing politicians to pay attention and transforming our national conversation about guns.[7]

Guns Kill People of Color

While we hear a lot about public mass shootings at schools, movie theaters, and malls, such events make up only 2 percent of all gun violence in America. We Americans are actually living in the midst of an epidemic of *everyday*, one-on-one gun violence.[1]

Approximately 80 percent of all gun homicides occur in urban areas and disproportionately claim lives in communities of color.[2] African American men are fourteen times more likely than non-Hispanic whites to die by homicide.[3] This same demographic makes up just 6 percent of the population but accounts for 51 percent of gun homicide victims. African American teens and twenty-somethings are eighteen times more likely than their white peers to be gun violence victims. An African American family has a 62 percent greater chance of losing a son to a bullet than to a car accident, and gun homicides reduce the average life expectancy of black Americans by 3.41 years. Comparatively, whites only lose half a year.[4]

As horrific as these numbers are, they sometimes obscure the true extent of the racial disparity, so consider this shocking statistic: in Milwaukee, Wisconsin, a black man between fifteen and twenty-four years of age was one hundred times more likely to be shot by a gun than a white non-Hispanic man of the same age in 2015.[5] One hundred times; that is revolting.

Hispanic Americans are also at a higher risk of gun violence. Hispanic whites are 2.6 times more likely to be murdered with guns than non-Hispanic whites, and younger Hispanics are hospitalized with firearm-related injuries 2.6 to 17.2 times more often than non-Hispanic whites.

The heart aches reading these numbers and imagining the lives lost, the families devastated, and the communities ruined. The mind demands to know the causes of such devastation.

Sociologists tell us that poverty, failing schools, economic inequality, and racial segregation are all strong predictors of higher rates of gun violence. When the institutions that encourage prosocial behavior break down, it's not hard to imagine why individuals would turn to underground economies and opportunities to survive. Often those illicit activities require a firearm.

But it would be wrong to assume that entire underserved communities are responsible for the violence. In fact, most gun crime is perpetrated by a small group of high-risk individuals in very specific geographical locations and social networks. In 2016, for instance, "50 percent of all the shootings in Chicago occurred in a handful of poorer neighborhoods, including Austin, Garfield Park, North and South Lawndale, Englewood, and West Pullman." The Brennan Center has found that just five neighborhoods in Chicago accounted for 10 percent of the national firearm homicide increase in 2016. The crime is "even more concentrated within those communities, occurring within just a few blocks," a study from Northwestern University found. Much of the carnage is fueled by interpersonal disputes that trigger retaliatory shootings within social networks where people are routinely exposed to violence and are increasingly likely to become its victims.[6] In particularly high-crime areas of Chicago, when someone in a certain social network is shot with a firearm, there is approximately a 20 percent chance that that person's friends and associates will also fall victim to gun violence within the next eighty days, researchers have found. A cycle of violence ensues.

To make matters worse, police are failing to solve these crimes and thus failing to deter people from committing them. "We are not catching anybody, [and that] means that you could shoot somebody with impunity in Chicago," Wesley Skogan, who studies crime at Northwestern University, explained during a March 2018 presentation on crime in Chicago. "An implication of that is you got to look out for yourself, a lot of gun carrying is defensive, people are worried about their own lives," and they are more likely to resort to "preemptive violence or retaliatory vengeance in order to model the effects of a criminal justice system which is now failing," he explained.[7]

A few individuals may perpetuate this violence, but it harms the entire community and feeds a cycle that is difficult to reverse. "One study found that for each homicide in a city, 70 residents flee, further hollowing out neighborhoods where tax revenues are already low and services insufficient," a report from Everytown for Gun Safety points out. In fact, "a single gunshot wound has a societal cost of about $1 million when all the consequences are added up," including depressed real estate prices, medical costs, diminished business activity, and lower economic growth. Estimates show that gun violence costs major cities billions of dollars every year.

Some of this killing also occurs at the hands of police. Police officers, after all, operate in the same world we do, a world where racial assumptions and stereotypes are pervasive. While the overwhelming majority of police officers are hardworking professionals, they perform their jobs with firearms, within a heavily armed gun culture that views weapons as the ultimate means of self-defense and promotes a stand-your-ground, shoot-first-ask-questions-later attitude. Maybe that's why an American between the ages of eighteen and twenty-nine is shot and killed by a police officer in the United States almost every day. Of those killed, 34 percent are African American, and at least 40 percent are unarmed.[8] Take institutional racism, add to it police brutality and a toxic gun culture, and you're left with thousands of unarmed black men shot dead in the prime of their lives.

DeJuan Patterson's story illustrates the intersection of law enforcement, guns, and race. Patterson, a native Baltimorean, was biking home from his job at Johns Hopkins Hospital in East Baltimore one night in 2005, when he was robbed at gunpoint and shot. He immediately went into shock. His head was bleeding, and he lost vision in one eye. When he regained consciousness, he found himself staring down the barrel of another gun: a police officer who saw DeJuan as a possible suspect and yelled obscenities at him, ordering him to get up off the ground. In a matter of minutes, he became, as he put it to me, both a gunshot victim and an alleged criminal.

It took DeJuan ten years to tell this story. These days, he tells it often, in hopes of drawing awareness to the ways gun violence in his community intersects with other issues faced by people of color: police brutality, lack of jobs and economic mobility, lack of help for mental health problems exacerbated by poverty, lack of access to quality education, and sometimes even lack of clean water. In 2011, DeJuan helped start the BeMore Group, an organization that hosts legal clinics, financial literacy classes, and meals with police officers and works with other nonprofits and governments to educate them about the challenges young people in their community face.[9] DeJuan describes his mission as working to find "a solution for the person in front of the gun as well as the person behind the gun." For him, guns are just one element of a whole constellation of interrelated problems. His work is a sober reminder of how high the stakes are and how pervasive gun violence has been for young people like him.

Everyday gun violence rarely attracts the kind of media coverage that mass shootings do. If you conduct a Google News search for shootings right after a highly publicized tragedy occurs, you will almost always find more articles about that single mass shooting than stories about the far more ubiquitous violence that happens every single day in America. A Google News search analysis performed by the Century Foundation think tank over the months before and after the Orlando Pulse nightclub shooting in 2016 revealed that the term "Orlando shooting" generated 14,747 news articles while "shootings in Chicago" yielded 262. Orlando "received sixty-five times more coverage than the Chicago shootings that have left thousands wounded and hundreds dead," the researchers found.[10] As an advocate once told me, the tone of the media coverage is also different. When black people die, it's a crime story. When whites die, it's a loss of life story.

There is hope that this paradigm is shifting, however. The marches that followed the school shooting in Parkland, Florida, managed to fuse the voices of those who have long lived with an everyday threat of gun violence with the survivors of mass tragedy, creating collective recognition of the scope of the problem. We as a society are beginning to acknowledge the undeniable intersection of gun violence and race. People in poor, urban, mixed-race communities often find themselves on both ends of a gun barrel and grapple with these realities every day.

Guns Kill Women and Children

"Where there are more guns, more women die," Dr. Deborah Azrael, a Harvard researcher, told *Salon* in 2015.[1] She's not wrong. Women are eleven times more likely to be murdered with guns in the United States than in other developed countries. In fact, 84 percent of all the female victims of gun violence in the developed world are American, even though American women make up just one-third of the total female population in the developed world.

In America, more than half of domestic violence murders of women between fifteen and twenty-nine years of age are committed by someone holding a gun.[2] And more than half of the time, the person responsible for murdering or physically harming a woman with a firearm is not a stranger or a burglar. The perpetrator is the woman's own intimate partner or a family member.

I will never forget the heart-wrenching story domestic abuse survivor Kate Ranta told to a group of protesters gathered in front of the NRA's headquarters in Fairfax, Virginia, just days after the Las Vegas mass shooting in October of 2017. I had traveled from DC to take part in the action, hand out signs to the crowd that read "fewer guns, safer communities," and broadcast some of the speakers through my Twitter account.

Ranta, who looked to be in her mid-thirties, with chin-length blond hair and a long-sleeved pink shirt, approached the podium with her young son William.

"My name is Kate Ranta and I'm coming up on the fifth anniversary of the night my ex-husband stalked me to my apartment, armed with a gun, a Beretta, 9mm, loaded with hollow point bullets, and shot directly at the door behind which my father and I were standing," she began. A noticeable hush fell over the crowd and I remember exhaling deeply as I stood and listened just a couple of feet away.

The bullets from her ex-husband's gun penetrated the door and he pushed his way into the apartment. "My right hand, it's my dominant hand, it exploded right in front of my face," Ranta said. "He walked over to my father and he shot him point blank in the side and I heard my father grunt and I thought he died."

Ranta herself was shot twice. She was crawling in her own blood, screaming and begging for her life. "I could literally feel the cold and I could feel myself dying," she told us.

Meanwhile, Ranta's son William, then four years old, witnessed everything. He was jumping up and down and screaming, trying to get his father to stop. "Don't do it, Daddy, don't shoot Mommy," he screamed out. The shooting stopped and Ranta, her father, and William escaped the apartment alive.

Just a year earlier, Ranta had done what domestic abuse survivors are always told to do: she took her son and left her abusive husband. She felt scared of him. The man had served in the Air Force and kept multiple firearms in their house. She took out a restraining order to keep him as far away as possible. "When he was served a temporary restraining order the police said they could go in, once he was served, and remove the firearms from the home, which they did, but then they proceeded to tell us that they can take all of the guns, but then he can go out the next day and get another gun, which is exactly what he did." Ranta's husband got a new gun, Googled "husband shooting wife," and went out to commit murder.

Federal law often fails to protect women from armed domestic abusers. Current or former boyfriends, for instance, who have been convicted of a domestic violence crime but have no children with their current partner and do not live with that partner, are permitted to own a firearm. Individuals who are convicted of misdemeanor stalking can also own a firearm.[3] This is despite the fact that domestic abuse is a key warning sign of future gun violence. An analysis by Everytown for Gun Safety of mass shootings from 2009 to 2016 found that the mass murderer had previously killed an intimate partner or other family members in 54 percent of instances.[4]

The mere presence of firearms in the home endangers women and in states where firearms are more widely available, women—like their male counterparts—have higher rates of suicide, homicide, and accidental gun death. African American women bear the brunt of this danger. They are three times as likely to die from a gun as white women and are twice as likely to be fatally shot by an intimate partner compared to white women.

A gun in the home during a domestic dispute increases by 500 percent the probability that the woman will be the victim of homicide or that the weapon will be used to threaten her in an act of nonfatal, but no less traumatic, domestic violence. Four and a half million women say that an intimate partner threatened them with a firearm—an astonishing statistic.[5] In fact, 554 American women are shot and killed by their romantic partners every single year, on average—a death every sixteen hours.[6]

Now, some women respond to the risks posed by America's "guns everywhere" culture by choosing to arm themselves for self-defense. I am in no position to judge or condemn women's decisions; as I argue later in the book, they should have that choice. However, less than half of 1 percent of women report having to actually use a gun for this purpose, and the data suggest that intimate partners threaten women with guns more often than women use them for protection.[7] Some data show that for every woman who uses a firearm in self-defense, eighty-three are murdered with a firearm by an intimate partner. A Harvard study of more than three hundred cases of sexual assault between 2007 and 2011 similarly found that not one attack was stopped by a firearm.

Ranta's son William is one of many young children impacted by guns in America. International studies have found that "91 percent of firearm deaths of children aged 0 to 14 years among all high-income countries worldwide occur in the United States."[8] Nineteen children die or are treated for gun-related wounds every single day in America. If the fatal wounds came about through homicide, the children are likely to be African American between the ages of thirteen and seventeen; if the cause of death is suicide, the children are likely to be in the same age group but white or Native American.

A mind-blowing study published in June 2017 in *Pediatrics*, the journal of the American Academy of Pediatrics, listed gunshot as the third leading cause of death for American children, outpacing causes like "pediatric congenital anomalies, heart disease, influenza and/or pneumonia, chronic lower respiratory disease, and cerebrovascular causes."[9] Approximately 1,300 children die from firearm-related injuries and 6,000 are treated for such injuries every single year in America, it found. And as we've seen, communities of color bear the brunt of these tragedies. "African American children have the highest rates of firearm mortality overall," the study's authors wrote. They are four times more likely to die from gun violence than Hispanic children and ten times more likely to die from guns than white or Asian American children.

We Are Killing Ourselves with Guns

Gun rights advocates often seek to downplay the carnage that fire-arms cause by pointing out that a significant share of gun deaths are suicides. According to the Centers for Disease Control and Prevention, nearly two-thirds of gun deaths are suicides.[1] White people living in rural areas are disproportionately affected. Between 2007 and 2016, young white Americans' gun suicide rate was 2.6 times higher than Hispanics', 1.7 times higher than African Americans', and 3.5 times higher than Asians'.[2]

These grim statistics are the result of many interconnected factors: poverty and lack of jobs, failure to identify warning signals early, and a limited health care system, especially for mental health. One overarching factor is often overlooked, however: the abundance and availability of guns in America.

Study after study has found that higher rates of gun ownership correspond with higher rates of suicide. A 2007 analysis of state household firearm ownership found that "males and females and people of all age groups were at higher risk for suicide if they lived in a state with high firearm prevalence." Individuals residing in states where guns were more available were almost twice as likely to commit suicide as those living in states where gun ownership was less popular—even though non-firearm suicides occurred at equal rates in both sets of states.[3]

Since 1999, the United States has been experiencing a dramatic increase in suicides. In June 2018, researchers found that the number of suicides has increased since then in forty-four states, and thirty states saw an increase of more than 30 percent.[4] The United States now has one of the world's highest rates of firearm suicides, 6.4 per 100,000 people (second only to Greenland).

People living in homes with firearms are no more likely to suffer from depression or substance abuse than people who live in houses without firearms. Individuals in crisis just have easy access to a tool that can end their lives more quickly and efficiently.

This should be common sense for the millions of Americans whose dieting strategy is a lot like the mantra my friend Errick drilled into my head when we started working out together. "If you keep good food in your fridge, you will eat good food," he told me over and over and over again. The technique places an obstacle between you and your impulses. It works because if your refrigerator is not already overflowing with pizza, you are less likely to go to great lengths to obtain pizza. The same principle applies to someone going through crisis: obstacles that interfere with an individual's suicidal impulse save lives. That is why cities that experience high numbers of suicides by people jumping off of bridges erect barriers to deter jumpers. The barriers decrease suicide rates at the barricaded bridges without increasing suicides on other bridges. Similarly, states with tougher gun restrictions see drops in firearm suicides without experiencing higher rates of suicide by other means. There is simply no displacement effect among those inclined to self-destruct in a moment of extreme despair. They tend to think better of it if the means of death are not readily at hand.

I must also point out that lesbian, gay, bisexual, and transgender people suffer from particularly high suicide rates and would benefit from stricter gun restrictions. Lesbian, gay, and bisexual youth are five times more likely to attempt suicide than their straight contemporaries. Between 10 and 20 percent of LGB people try to kill themselves over the course of their lives; the rate seems to be highest during the teenage years. In 2015, research found that a staggering 40 percent of high school students who are gay, lesbian, bisexual, or questioning their orientation seriously contemplated killing themselves; almost 25 percent had actually attempted suicide.[5] For transgender people, the numbers are even higher, 41 percent say they have tried to kill themselves at some point.[6] This is just one way that bigotry kills, and unfortunately the availability of guns in America makes a suicide attempt far more likely to be successful.

How I Became a Fewer-Guns Activist

I came to the gun control movement for the same reason I suspect you picked up this book: I was pissed off. I was pissed off by the toll that gun violence has taken in our country and by craven politicians who claim to pray for the survivors while propping up the NRA and perpetuating a gun culture that exists nowhere else in the developed world. I wanted to do something about it.

I was born in the Soviet Union and eventually made it to America with my family to escape the persecution of Jews. It was hard to succeed, even to get by, for Soviet Jews. We faced limitations in education, employment, and life in general. My parents became targets of horrific anti-Semitism as they were coming of age, and I myself remember young children, no older than five or six, mocking me for being Jewish as we all lay in the children's section of a Soviet hospital. (I ended up there after managing to tip over an upright piano onto myself.)

As immigrants, my family moved all around New Jersey in search of better opportunities, communities, and schools. The experience of having to assimilate to an entirely different culture and language sparked my interest in the policies and attitudes that shape our society and give meaning to our culture.

I first became interested in politics during the 2000 election. I had just started high school in Livingston, New Jersey, when Al Gore and George W. Bush began campaigning for president. Something about that race forced me to start changing the channel on our TV from MTV's *Total Request Live* to CNN and MSNBC. At first I caught only brief glimpses of the news, but halfway through that year, I knew far more about the candidates' education, health, and, yes, gun policies than the ranking of pop music videos. I became the kid who would stay after class to talk to his teacher about the presidential race, and as a result, I'd miss my bus home and have to walk. One day, as I was scanning through the radio stations on my bright yellow Sony Walkman, I stumbled on a talk show hosted by a man named Bob Grant, broadcasting from WOR, New York, at 710 on the AM dial. He was a far-right conservative talk-show host. I later learned that he was considered the godfather of conservative talk radio and a mentor to contemporary radio stars like Rush Limbaugh, Sean Hannity, and Mark Levin. I was hooked, but not by Grant's political ideology. I couldn't get behind his hatred of immigrants or his support for an economic system that strongly favored the rich. I was mesmerized by Grant's ability to carefully construct arguments and woo his audience to his beliefs. I was attracted by the power and utility of political persuasion.

Suddenly my innocent political conversations with teachers turned into full-blown political debates, and I became a most loyal listener of conservative talk radio and viewer of cable TV news. By the time I entered my junior year of high school, I would steal newspapers from the school library and read them in gym class, highlighting or underlining key facts or arguments. I wanted to grow up to convince people of things. I wanted to mold arguments that would rid us of injustices like the ones I experienced as a young child growing up in the Soviet Union and later as an immigrant in America.

I did not apply those skills to gun control until late 2015. By then, I had been working in politics for nearly a decade, most of that time as a reporter for *ThinkProgress*, a news site run by the Center for

American Progress, a progressive think tank in Washington, DC. I covered many of the policies that animated the Obama years, from health care reform to the repeal of Don't Ask, Don't Tell, as well as his administration's efforts to reform the immigration system. My first exposure to guns as seen through the lens of politics happened as a result of tragedy—the December 14, 2012, massacre at Sandy Hook Elementary School in Newtown, Connecticut. As I followed the administration's failed attempt to expand background checks and pass an assault weapons ban, I became familiar with the general arguments on both sides of the debate.

Then, on December 2, 2015, a man and a woman walked into a community center in San Bernardino, California, and killed fourteen people with four semiautomatic weapons.[1] They had committed the 366th mass shooting of 2015. Almost immediately, I began receiving news alerts and push notifications on my phone. I tried to ignore them, as I was busy shooting a video with a colleague. At the end of the day, I sat back down at my computer and read my Twitter feed, the best place to receive up-to-the-minute updates on breaking news events. I had made a column in the platform to track tweets from members of Congress. By early afternoon on December 2, it was overflowing with "thoughts and prayers" for the shooting victims, their survivors, and the first responders who rushed to the scene.

I remember slamming my fist down on my desk in anger. My heart rate quickened. I felt a familiar wave of rage rise up inside of me.

It was a feeling I first experienced when I was six years old, briefly living in Israel with my family. We lived in the country for two years in the early 1990s before finally immigrating to the United States. I was sitting at Hanukkah dinner hosted by an Orthodox Jewish family. Israeli Jews would often host *olim* (new immigrants to Israel) on high holidays to help acclimate new immigrants to the country and its traditions. Everyone was exchanging gifts. I received a few small things, but then the patriarch of the Orthodox family told me that my stepfather had gotten me a brand-new red bicycle. I couldn't believe it! We had left the Soviet Union just a year ago and had been living in a group house with other Soviet Jewish families. My parents had opened a café, but even at my young age, I knew that money was tight. I could never imagine asking for anything flashy, much less something as expensive as a new bike. And here, they had gone out of their way to get me one!

The rest of the dinner became a blur. All I could think about was the bike and riding it all around our little neighborhood. I knew my ever protective mom wouldn't let me get too far by myself, but all I really wanted was to feel the wind against my face. As soon as we left the dinner, I asked my stepdad about the bike. He smiled down at me, rubbed my head, and said, "Oh no, that guy was just kidding." My heart dropped. I felt a mixture of disappointment, sadness, and anger—anger at the man at that dinner table for filling me with false hope, tricking me, and making me feel like a fool. I somehow felt bad for ever believing I would get a bike in the first place. That experience woke something inside of me, and I would come to recognize the same feelings anytime someone tried to pull the wool over my eyes. I loathed the disappointment of that day, and I still feel rage on behalf of people who experience something similar.

I thought about that bike as I tracked "thoughts and prayers" from the same members of Congress who had voted against legislative measures to prevent gun violence in the aftermath of the shooting at Sandy Hook Elementary School. They were exploiting a tragic moment to fool their constituents into believing they cared enough to do something to prevent public mass shootings, despite knowing full well that they would not.

Almost instinctively, I started to send angry tweets at members of Congress tweeting their thoughts and prayers. I began with the ones I recognized as opponents of the background-check bill that failed after the Newtown shooting. I did this over and over again. I told these lawmakers that when they had a chance to prevent such carnage and vote for a measure that would at least make incidents of gun violence less likely, they failed. Instead they chose to demonize the measure, misrepresent it, outright lie about it, and lead an orchestrated campaign to defeat it. They did all this not because they were representing the interests of their constituents; to the contrary, the overwhelming majority of their voters support universal background checks.[2] They did it because they were afraid of the political influence and clout of the gun industry and its energized supporters, and because they were being paid by that gun lobby to represent the interests of gun manufacturers for whom any restrictions represent a loss of sales. These tweets felt raw and emotional. Before long, I had responded to every member I could identify as an opponent of gun reform.

About an hour into this tweetstorm, I decided I needed to calm down and blow off some steam. I took a break and walked to a Cross-Fit class across the street, letting my mind and body work through all of the anger. Before I left, I noticed some people on Twitter cautioning me against discussing policy so soon after a mass shooting. I remember thinking, *Those guys should notify me when it's "appropriate" to discuss solutions.* The country never gets around to a genuine conversation about policy. Instead, we engage in a short, divisive debate that generates no real change.

At the end of gym class, I considered going straight home, but my curiosity got the better of me. I wanted to see if more lawmakers were tweeting out their "thoughts and prayers" and how my tweets calling them out were being received. I ran back to my office on the second floor, drenched in sweat, as I remember, and woke my computer back up by tapping on the mouse repeatedly. As the screen came back to life, I could see the Members of Congress column scrolling feverishly; they were still at it, pretending to care. My tweets, meanwhile, had taken off—big time. While some insisted that I was "politicizing" a shooting, many more cheered me on and told their followers to follow me. This support sparked an idea. I realized that many people shared my frustration with congressional inaction on gun control and that they, too, blamed special interests and our broken campaign finance rules for the problem. What if there was a way to accentuate that feeling and show how that money shaped lawmakers' behavior?

A colleague directed me to Open Secrets, a site that tracks political contributions. I clicked over to the NRA and saw pages and pages of giving. Before long, I had set up a new process for tweeting out at the "thoughts and prayers" members of Congress. Whenever a member of Congress who opposed gun control would tweet that he or she was praying for the victims of the shooting, I would methodically add up how much that person received from the NRA on a scrap piece of paper and tweet that total, with a message along the lines of, "Rep. Long received $10,000 from @NRA, so he'll only think and pray about gun violence; he won't actually do anything to stop it."

When Senate Majority Leader Mitch McConnell tweeted, "The senseless loss of innocent life in #SanBernardino defies explanation," I reminded him that he had taken more than $900,000 from the NRA in his last election.[3] I did the same thing to Paul Ryan's condolence tweet, informing my followers that he, too, had taken money from the NRA to keep the victims in his "thoughts and prayers."[4]

Those tweets became even more popular, logging hundreds of retweets and likes within minutes. To me, the dollar amounts represented not only the money the NRA spent on behalf of a lawmaker or against the lawmaker's opponent, but also the power of the lobby to motivate its members to make calls, send letters, and do physical lobbying in the lawmaker's offices. My follower count began to grow exponentially. I had started the day at approximately twelve thousand followers. By eight or nine that night, I was gaining about

ten new followers a minute. My friends and colleagues began email-
ing me, saying they were seeing what I was doing and urging me to
keep going. Someone from Twitter reached out to suggest that I tag
the names of the lawmakers I was shaming in my tweets so that they
would feel the impact in their mentions.

Before I knew it, my work caught the attention of cable news pro-
ducers. I closed the day with an emotional appearance on MSNBC,
which featured my tweets, and over the next several days, I continued the Twitter action, as some lawmakers introduced gun-reform
measures and the majority of our elected officials voted them down.

One of the beauties of democracy is accessibility. If you want to
understand a pressing public issue, you can. If, after you learn about
it, you want to change how the government responds to it, there are
processes through which you can do that as well. You can educate
yourself about the issue and then add value to the discussion in a
way that attracts other people to contribute. You can tweet, you can
organize your friends and neighbors, you can attend meetings with
decision makers, and you can vote. The list goes on. My decision
to start tweeting was rooted in raw emotion. I used the only tool
I had—my Twitter account. My message resonated because I was
meeting people where they were. I was tapping into public frustration about congressional inaction to reduce gun violence by quanti-
fying the inaction. I was adding data to people's emotion.

I didn't shut up after San Bernardino. Tragically, I had many more
opportunities to tap into this frustration and expose hypocrisy in
our modern-day public square. Just a little over six months after
those first tweets, a gunman stormed into the Pulse nightclub in
Orlando, Florida, and killed forty-nine people.

I woke up to the news that Sunday morning and spent the next
eight hours at my kitchen table, glued to Twitter, which was again
overflowing with "thoughts and prayers." I started tweeting out at

lawmakers again. This time, I could Google my old tweets from San Bernardino to avoid recalculating the total contribution number. I remember that feeling awful and incredibly depressing.

By then, I had eighty thousand Twitter followers. Shaming lawmakers and corporations who do business with the NRA is pretty popular. I appeared on numerous TV shows and even earned several shout-outs from Kim Kardashian, Mindy Kaling, John Legend, and other celebrities from outside of the political arena.

From my anger and the Twitter platform, an opportunity was born. I recognized that Americans responded to my simple argument: *special interest money and influence are undermining our safety and taking our lives.* And as I learned more about the gun-safety movement, I recognized that my approach and skill set as an advocate could add value to the existing voices calling for change. I was very moved by the persistence, strength, and expertise of those who had dedicated their professional lives to reducing gun violence, including organizations like the Brady Campaign, Everytown for Gun Safety, and Giffords, as well as my strategic and creative colleagues from the Center for American Progress, particularly Chelsea Parsons, Tim Daly, and Arkadi Gerney. In the weeks following my tweets, they served as my orientation leaders to the broader movement, teaching me everything I needed to know about its policy and advocacy. Through their tutelage, I recognized that the movement lacked advocates and organizations that called for reforms that might not be politically viable yet but could make real change in the future as people's outrage builds. We needed to develop a bold message promulgated by voices that could go toe-to-toe with the NRA and work like hell to weaken it. My tweets also convinced me that Americans were ahead of their risk-averse political leaders on the gun issue and were ready to get behind solutions and advocacy campaigns that focused on significantly limiting the availability of guns.

Out of that realization, I co-founded Guns Down America. We

formed around the same ideas that drove my tweets: holding people in power—in politics and business—accountable for flooding our communities with guns and being complicit in the deaths of thousands of Americans every single year. There are many voices in this fight; Guns Down America is the first dedicated to the singular mission of building a world with fewer guns.

I continue to tweet NRA contribution amounts after every single publicized mass shooting. The tweets are no longer as popular as they were in 2015, and many people have begun taking similar digital actions. To me, that is a sign of success, a small building block for our ultimate goal of building communities with fewer guns. As more people shame lawmakers for taking NRA contributions and attribute their votes against gun-safety legislation to those contributions and the political power they represent, the less likely we are to support them or to believe their phony arguments.

One other piece of progress came about as a result of that initial tweetstorm: the death of the "It's too soon to talk about solutions" argument. When I first started working on the gun issue, that claim was bandied around by Democrats and Republicans alike, as folks sought to soften the blow of inaction by postponing the conversation about policy to another day. After the tweetstorm, that argument has been confined to the echo chamber of the gun lobby. Today, Democratic lawmakers insert policy into the public conversation within minutes of a shooting. And they should. We always talk about tightening or changing laws in the aftermath of a terrorist incident. Why not have that conversation if the weapon used to inflict that terror is a gun? It took legislators less than a week to introduce a bill that penalizes airlines for recklessly transporting pets after a woman was forced to put her dog (in a TSA-approved carrier) in an overhead luggage bin, where the animal suffocated. Do dogs really matter more than humans to certain lawmakers?

———

During the summer of 2018, I was sitting in a swanky New York bar that was once a movie theater, meeting an acquaintance who works in conservative media. The man grew up in England, and although he politically identifies as right of center and, I suspect, would quibble with parts of this book, he admitted that he could not understand Americans' fascination with firearms. "Why are Americans so obsessed with guns?" he asked me. I had been thinking about this question for years, but nobody had forced me to answer it so directly before.

"I think guns have been central to American history, from the colonial era on. Early Americans used firearms to dominate the people and the land; they used their firearms to win independence," I said. "So firearms have always had a place in our folklore." "But more recently," I continued, "the gun lobby and the gun industry imbued gun ownership with a political meaning and identity that they manipulated to gain political power and sell more guns."

My friend nodded along respectfully. As I sat there thinking about my answer, I realized that my argument for fewer guns was rooted in a far more conservative interpretation of the Second Amendment and the intents of the men who wrote it than my friend's audience would ever accept today. The eighteenth-century authors of the Second Amendment sought to build a new country with fewer guns. In the pages that follow, I describe why and how they failed so miserably.

The Founding Fathers Wanted a Country with Fewer Guns

In 2018, President Donald Trump addressed the NRA's annual conference for the second time as a sitting president. He was only the second sitting president to do so. In 1983, then president Ronald Reagan became the first.

Both Reagan and Trump had at one time supported a ban on military-style assault weapons, a completely rational policy that the gun lobby views as a gun grab. Reagan came out for the reform ten years after he addressed the NRA; Trump endorsed it before he entered national politics. Reagan delivered his remarks with trademark passion and conviction; Trump rattled off a list of platitudes before launching into a recitation of his political conquests.

But both men delivered a similar message thirty-five years apart, and both distorted history.

Reagan said in 1983: "And by the way, the Constitution does not say that government shall decree the right to keep and bear arms. The Constitution says, 'the right of the people to keep and bear Arms, shall not be infringed.'"[1]

Trump said in 2018: "Since the first generation of Americans stood strong at Concord, each generation to follow has answered the call to defend freedom in their time. That is why we are here today: To defend freedom for our children. To defend the liberty of all Americans. And to defend the right of a free and sovereign people to keep and bear arms."[2]

Reagan and Trump framed the Second Amendment as an absolute right to own and carry firearms. The men (and yes, they were all men) who wrote our Constitution, however, saw that Second Amendment right to bear arms as a civic responsibility that white men had to meet in order to serve and protect their communities. The amendment was rooted in notions of responsible and ordered citizenship and was never seen as an unlimited and unregulatable right. The modern view of the Second Amendment articulated by Reagan and Trump, the one that views almost all gun regulations as contradictory to the right to bear arms, did not take hold until many years later, invented and perpetuated by a gun lobby intent on helping the firearms industry sell more guns.

For centuries, Americans had accepted and even promoted strict gun controls.

During the Revolutionary War period, for instance, the colonists heavily regulated firearms within a militia structure. Service was mandatory, and the militias were made up of white male landowners, who were required to carry and obtain their own firearms—guns they used to strip Native Americans of their land and rule enslaved Africans. To facilitate this dirty work—and ensure that guns did not fall into the "wrong" hands—early Americans employed stringent gun regulations. The early colonies required that guns be registered and inspected.[3] Regulation of firearms in the colonies both during and after independence included policing powers over nonmilitary use of the weapons. Colonial governments tracked citizens' firearms, and militiamen faced stiff penalties if they failed to report to muster. While many individual colonies had rules governing the storage of gunpowder, some regulations went even further.

Boston residents were not permitted to store a loaded firearm in their home, and individuals faced stiff penalties for violating this prohibition. Boston, along with New York, prohibited the firing of guns within city limits. Rhode Island conducted a house-by-house census of gun owners.[4] Pennsylvania law allowed the government to disarm individuals deemed insufficiently loyal to the state.

By the time the thirteen states came together in Philadelphia for the Constitutional Convention in 1787, four state constitutions protected the right to bear arms within a militia, but only Pennsylvania allowed broader ownership. (Given its high number of pacifist Quakers, the state could not form a standing militia and had to rely on armed individuals for protection.)

Most importantly, all of these early state constitutions described the right to bear arms as a *civic obligation*: citizens were required to arm themselves in order to participate in a militia that could protect them from foreign armies and internal threats. This understanding of self-defense was rooted in the English Bill of Rights of 1689, wherein the government tightly regulated firearms. The American colonists followed that norm, bearing arms "for the defence of the State" (North Carolina, Article XVII) or "for the common defence" (Massachusetts, Article XVII).[5]

We spend a lot of time debating the particulars of the Second Amendment today, but it may surprise you to learn that the right to bear arms was not particularly important to the men who penned the Constitution. They did not include it in their original draft, nor was there any great public clamoring for such a provision in the fiery debates that followed the Constitutional Convention. To the extent that guns were discussed at all, the debate focused on the merits of state-run militias versus a national standing army. Before the Convention, states had controlled and regulated their own militias. The authors of the new document sought to put the federal government in charge. This change caused great divisions.

One camp of delegates—the Federalists—feared that state-run citizen militias would be ill equipped to deal with future threats. They wanted a professional nationwide armed force. Other delegates—the Anti-Federalists—argued that Congress could abuse its power, disarm the state militias, and strip landowners of their rights. Eventually, the Federalists and Anti-Federalists agreed to a compromise: the federal government would be given the authority "To provide for organizing, arming, and disciplining, the Militia, and for governing such Part of them as may be employed in the Service of the United States," while the states controlled military training and the appointment of military officers.[6]

The Philadelphia Convention adjourned with that compromise, without any language about the "right to bear arms," and the founders sent the document to special conventions held within state legislatures for ratification.[7] Nine out of thirteen states had to approve the Constitution for the document to go into effect. The newly proposed order unleashed feverish debates all over the country.

Early Americans penned essays and pamphlets arguing about the role of government and its size in daily life. But here too, they spent almost no time debating the gun question.

In Massachusetts, the state convention actually rejected the statement that the "Constitution be never construed to authorize Congress . . . to prevent the people of the United States, who are peaceable citizens, from keeping their own arms." In Pennsylvania, a provision "that the people have a right to bear arms for the defense of themselves and their own state, or for the purpose of killing game; and no law shall be passed for disarming the people or any of them, unless for crimes committed, or real danger of public injury from individuals" was similarly voted down. That clause allowed for significant police regulation of firearms, but it was still lampooned by the leaders of the day. Noah Webster, the political writer and "father of American scholarship and education," asked sarcastically if Congress should not include language "that Congress shall never restrain any inhabitant of America from eating and drinking, at seasonable times, or prevent his lying on his left side, in a long winter's night, or even on his back, when he is fatigued by lying on his right."[8]

In other words, the minority view that the Constitution should explicitly allow for a right to self-defense never picked up any significant steam, and its adherents made no campaign to advance it.

So how did the Bill of Rights come to include the Second Amendment? It originated from one of the nation's first attempts to satisfy a political constituency!

The Constitution's chief author—James Madison—had a problem. He wanted to win a congressional seat in Virginia, but he needed the votes of white southern Baptists to do so. What did they want? After years of oppression by the Episcopal Church, they demanded a guarantee that the new American government would never prioritize one religion over another. As Michael Waldman, author of *The Second Amendment: A Biography*, put it, "Madison found himself one of the first American politicians to pirouette, in the course of a campaign, from a deeply held view to its opposite—all the while insisting (and trying to convince himself) that he had not changed his view at all. The Bill of Rights was born of a pander to a noisy interest group in a single congressional district."[9]

Madison did indeed initially oppose significantly changing the Constitution, arguing that enumerating specific rights would not prevent governments from trampling them and could disrupt the delicate balance of power between the federal government and the states as laid out in the document. Political expediency, however, convinced him to meet the Baptists' demand for an amendment guaranteeing religious freedom. Madison explained his change of mind: "It is my sincere opinion that the Constitution ought to be revised, and that the first Congress meeting under it ought to prepare and recommend to the States for ratification, the most satisfactory provisions for all essential rights, particularly the rights of

Conscience in the fullest latitude, the freedom of the press, trials by jury, security against general warrants &c."[10]

Note that Madison's list did not initially include a "right to bear arms," though as he drafted the Bill of Rights, he incorporated language from the recommendations sent by the states' ratification conventions. Those amendments included provisions about a right to bear arms within the context of a militia and did not appear to endorse an individual right to bear arms, even for hunting or self-defense.[11]

Madison's amendment echoed that sentiment, and after some revisions, it was codified into the twenty-seven words of the Second Amendment: "A well regulated Militia, being necessary to the security of a free State, the right of the people to keep and bear Arms, shall not be infringed."

Consider this amendment piece by piece:

"A well regulated militia": The founders were concerned about protecting the militia from the dangers of a centralized standing army as the phrase "the security of a free State" suggests. The first clause of the amendment qualifies the right articulated within it.

"A free State": Every time that phrase is used in the Constitution it refers to individual states, not the government as a whole.

"The people": The founders used this phrase to mean not individual persons, but rather the body politic, the people as a whole. During the ratification debate in Virginia, speakers used the phrase "the people" fifty times when discussing the militia. Every single mention referred to Virginians as a group, not as individuals.

"Keep and bear arms": If you search the phrase "right to bear arms" in the *Congressional Record*, you won't find a single mention outside of the context of the military. Searching a database of all the writings and papers of our founding fathers (Washington, Adams, Jefferson, Hamilton, Franklin, and Madison) also reveals that the "right to bear arms" referred only to the formation of militias.[12]

In the eighteenth century, the Second Amendment was about

militias and musters. It was not about the politics of rugged individualism or a God-given right to own as many firearms as possible. Understanding of the amendment evolved in the decades that followed, as our interpretation of the Constitution adapted to changing times. Yet the "right to bear arms" almost always reflected a collective spirit rather than an individual obligation, a duty that could be regulated to address concerns of public safety. A group of colonial historians explained it succinctly: "The authors of the Second Amendment would be flabbergasted to learn that in endorsing the republican principle of a well-regulated militia, they were also precluding restrictions on such potentially dangerous property as firearms, which governments had always regulated when there was 'real danger of public injury from individuals.'"[13]

During the nineteenth century, state militias began to give way to standing armies, and as the United States expanded west, violence increased. An organization dedicated to improving the marksmanship of American soldiers formed; it evolved into an association dedicated to undermining all gun regulations throughout the country. Before long, this group would launch a multimillion-dollar campaign to rewrite the history of the Second Amendment and distort the writings of our founding fathers to fit its message and political agenda.

The NRA: Birth of a Lobby

Throughout the late nineteenth and early twentieth centuries, the public face of the National Rifle Association was the gun-loving hobbyist who collected, restored, lovingly oiled, and would not shut up about his beautiful guns. Multiply him by a couple of thousand, and you have a pretty clear picture of what the organization looked like at first. Rather than insisting that every man, woman, and child (yes, child!) should own a gun—as it would nearly a century later—the NRA of our great-great-grandparents wanted to make sure that people who owned guns knew how to use them.

The NRA was established in 1871 in the aftermath of the Civil War, when technological innovation—particularly breech-loading guns and metal cartridge ammunition—allowed shooters, for the very first time, to aim and actually hit a desired target. American men needed to be trained to use the new technology, and the founders, Colonel William C. Church and General George Wingate, set out to improve American marksmanship. They envisioned the National Guard running a get-better-at-shooting association but realized that private enterprise could support the effort more quickly.

Still, those early years involved lots and lots of government assistance. Church and Wingate gratefully accepted New York's offer to host shooting contests at its rifle range at a place called Creedmoor, in Queens in New York City, now the site of a psychiatric hospital for

severely mentally ill patients. Once New York withdrew its support—
the state's optimistic governor, Alonzo Cornell, believed that "there
will be no war in my time or in the time of my children"—the federal
government aided the NRA by giving away hundreds of thousands of
surplus guns to its clubs at cost and partnered with the association on
marksmanship training and competitions.

These recreational gun enthusiasts did not see the Second Amendment as the bedrock of the entire American experiment, as their
successors do. The NRA of your grandparents' childhood privately
urged its members to oppose many gun restrictions, but it publicly sought to present itself as a willing partner in limiting crimes
through firearm regulation. While it would shed this compromising
attitude in the years ahead, its messaging to its members has been
remarkably consistent from the very beginning, even though it did
not initially cite the Second Amendment.

In 1911, the NRA opined on a state regulation in New York that
required police licenses for firearms. Writing in its magazine to
members, the lobby complained that additional licensing and other
restrictions "make it very difficult for an honest man and a good
citizen to obtain them," arguing that "such laws have the effect of
arming the bad man and disarming the good one."[1] Sound familiar?

In the 1920s, just as automobiles began to populate our streets,
the NRA weighed in on another growing phenomenon: criminals
with guns using cars to commit crimes and then quickly flee the
scene. An article published in the organization's magazine, *American
Rifleman*, argued that cars were to blame for increasing rates of gun
violence. "It's the automobile that's making the going tough for the
police—not the one-hand gun." These examples demonstrate the
early use of two modern-day NRA tactics: insist that gun regulations will disarm only law-abiding individuals to the advantage of
criminals, and then blame anything but the prevalence of guns for

the violence, no matter how ridiculous the argument. In the 1920s, it was the car. Today it's video games and Ritalin.

Nevertheless, this younger NRA did wear a far gentler and agreeable face in public than it does today. When three-time sport-shooting Olympic gold medalist Karl T. Frederick appeared before Congress to testify about the 1934 National Firearms Act, a measure that severely restricted access to machine guns and sawed off shot guns, he bragged about how the NRA was already working to make it harder for Americans to purchase firearms.

He said, "I have been giving this subject of firearms regulations study and consideration over a period of 15 years, and my suggestions . . . have resulted in the adoption in many States of regulatory provisions." Some of those provisions—adopted at the time in Washington, DC, and in several states—now read like a gun-safety advocate's agenda. Gun dealers could be licensed only at the discretion of police; they were required to keep detailed records of all transactions and provide, within hours of the purchase, a buyer's personal information to the authorities.

Frederick did not enthusiastically support the 1934 federal law; he told Congress that states would probably be best equipped to implement these regulations. But he did offer lawmakers constructive criticism for how to improve the federal bill, and he endorsed the general notion of gun safety.

"I do not believe in the general promiscuous toting of guns," Frederick said. "I think it should be sharply restricted and only under licenses." The NRA head reviewed the bill with lawmakers almost line by line, and when a representative asked him if the proposed law "interferes in any way with the right of a person to keep and bear arms" or violates any part of the Constitution, he responded, "I have not given it any study from that point of view." NRA executive vice president Milton Reckford was even more direct about the need to restrict the ownership of certain kinds of firearms, telling Congress,

"We believe that the machine gun, submachine gun, sawed-off shotgun, and dangerous and deadly weapons could all be included in any kind of a bill, and no matter how drastic, we will support it."[2]

However, the NRA's public remarks bore little resemblance to the way it portrayed the bill to its members. It wouldn't discover the power of Second Amendment fundamentalism until the 1970s, but its antipathy to most gun restrictions was never too far below the surface. In a May 1934 publication, the organization warned that the National Firearms Act's "viciousness lies in the opportunity for disarmament by subterfuge" and ran editorials with titles like "Keep Those Letters and Telegrams Coming," urging its eighty thousand or so members to "communicate [their opposition] at once by telegram and special-delivery letter with both their Representatives and their Senators in Washington."[3] So many members responded that Assistant Attorney General Joseph Keenan claimed that lawmakers felt "emasculated" by the reaction.

This innovation, the direct-contact campaign, would prove pivotal to the lobby's power over lawmakers. Around the same time, the NRA also transformed its recreational rifle clubs into political organizations to oppose gun restrictions, seeking to maximize public pressure.

Despite the NRA's opposition, the measure passed. Five years later, the U.S. Supreme Court took up the question of the law's constitutionality, which the lobby never questioned. The Supreme Court upheld the National Firearms Act, agreeing unanimously with the argument that the Constitution's Second Amendment right to bear arms "is not one which may be utilized for private purposes, but only one which exists where the arms are borne in the militia or some other military organization provided for by law and intended for the protection of the state." That view held for sixty-nine years, until the landmark *District of Columbia v. Heller* decision in 2008.

Throughout the 1940s and 1950s, the NRA operated as a quasi-governmental organization, and the federal government avoided any new gun restrictions. The lobby hired a former senior manager from the Internal Revenue Service, Franklin L. Orth, to represent its interests, organized government-sponsored national shooting matches, and helped run a federal program to promote firearm safety and training. Still, warnings about disarmament were never off the agenda.

In an April 1948 editorial published in the *American Rifleman*, the organization argued, "The pattern of Communist action is now well established. . . . [In Communist states], all shooting clubs were closed by legal decree. All privately-owned small arms were taken into 'safekeeping' by the police. . . . All patriotic citizens had been disarmed when the arms registration lists were seized by Hitler's Fifth Column. . . . How can anyone, squarely facing the contemporary record, seek or support laws which would require American citizens to register their privately owned firearms with any municipal, state, or federal agency?"

The NRA would soon have to put the power of that argument to the test.

On November 22, 1963, Lee Harvey Oswald assassinated President John F. Kennedy using a Mannlicher-Carcano rifle he purchased for $19.95 through an ad in *American Rifleman*. The killing shocked the nation. It also spurred Congress to consider legislation banning mail-order firearms, which were easy to acquire and, as a result, were frequently used in crime. The NRA facilitated these purchases through its network of publications, but few know that it actually helped develop the ammunition that ultimately killed the president.

After World War II, as the United States began arming anti-Communist groups in Greece, it worked with the NRA to design and manufacture ammunition that would improve the accuracy of certain rifles. That ammunition eventually made its way into the U.S. domestic market and into the barrel of the Oswald gun. When Orth learned of the connection, he allegedly told a Senate staffer, "Please don't tell anybody because we don't want to be hung with having been involved in producing the ammunition that killed the President."[4]

If the NRA felt any guilt for allowing Oswald to easily arm himself, it did not show it. For several years, the lobby urged its members to oppose multiple bills that sought to severely restrict the interstate sale of firearms. The NRA argued that such limits would ban "the private ownership of all guns," and that lie successfully held off multiple federal gun restrictions.

I should note here that the politics of gun control in the 1960s cannot be divorced from the racism that pervaded American society. Many white leaders felt threatened by the social-justice movements of the era and sought to use gun restrictions as a way to prevent African Americans from acquiring firearms. For some white leaders, the justification for gun restrictions sounded like this quote from Chicago mayor Richard J. Daley: "You've got people out there, especially the nonwhites, are buying guns right and left. You got guns and rifles and pistols and everything else," Daley said. "There's no registration. There isn't a damn thing."[5]

But soon, several high-profile gun deaths proved that the power of the NRA and its members to defeat restrictive laws was not without limit.

First, Martin Luther King was gunned down in a Memphis, Tennessee, hotel in April 1968. Two months later, Robert F. Kennedy was killed with a .22 handgun in Los Angeles, California.

Thirteen days after that, on June 19, 1968, President Lyndon B. Johnson signed into law a bill to ban the interstate sale and ship-

ment of handguns. He later expanded the ban to include rifles and
shotguns and instituted prohibitions against most felons and people
who were found to be mentally incompetent from purchasing firearms. Caving to public pressure, the NRA generally supported the
Gun Control Act of 1968. "The measure as a whole appears to be
one that sportsmen of America can live with," the leadership said at
the time.

That statement did not sit well with a small group of extremists
inside the organization, and it would prove pivotal in transforming
the NRA.

On May 21, 1977, a stout, bald man named Harlon Bronson
Carter wrested control of the NRA from the so-called old guard
that had supported the 1968 law. Carter's gripe? The old leaders did
not do enough to defend the Second Amendment. They had failed
to stop the Gun Control Act of 1968. In 1975 in the NRA *Fact Book
on Firearms Control*, they had written that the Second Amendment
is "of limited practical utility" as an argument against gun restrictions.[6] They were planning to move the NRA headquarters from
Washington, DC, to Colorado Springs, Colorado, to focus more
on sport shooting and hunting. They had even fired Carter and
eighty-four other staff members in preparation for that move out
west.

The disgruntled former employees soon formed the Federation
of the NRA with the goal of ousting the old NRA leaders and taking over. At the organization's annual convention a year later, the
group succeeded. The old guard, who, in the view of Carter, had not
worked hard enough to defeat gun regulations, was out.

The fundamentalists, known as the new guard, quickly established defense of the Second Amendment as a guiding principle for
the NRA and greatly increased funding to the organization's lobbying arm. The NRA as we know it today was born.

Perhaps it's no surprise that the organization's new, more radical views were propagated by a radical man.

A native Texan, Harlon Carter had his first consequential experience with a firearm at age fourteen. In 1931, the Carter family lived in the border town of Laredo, Texas, home to a large Mexican population. One day, Carter's mother suspected that a group of Mexican boys hanging around the house had stolen her car. Young Carter sprang into action. He grabbed his shotgun and went to look for the boys, finding them at a nearby swimming hole. He demanded they follow him back to his home. They refused, and fifteen-year-old Ramón Casiano pulled out a knife. In the skirmish that ensued, the future NRA leader—whose mentees would go on to develop the slogan "The only thing that can stop a bad guy with a gun is a good guy with a gun"—shot and killed Casiano. Carter was convicted of murder and sentenced to three years in prison, but he served only two.

As writer Laura Smith put it in a 2017 piece on Carter's life, "The scene had everything that would come to define the organization: home and family, a fervent sense of self-protection, vigilantism, and standing your ground," adding that the incident "exemplifies the association's tacit approval of race-based violence and white impunity."[7]

Carter's embrace of violent racism defined his adult professional life, too, and set the course of the NRA for years to come. In 1950, Carter became chief of the U.S. Border Patrol and presided over Operation Wetback—the biggest mass deportation in American history.[8] The operation, occasioned by a breakdown in negotiations over the legal sponsorship of Mexican workers in the United States, used military tactics to deport more than a million workers across the border. Carter described the effort to the *Los Angeles Times* as an "all-out war to hurl . . . Mexican wetbacks back into Mexico."[9]

As you can tell, Carter was never subtle about his bigotry or his desire to oppress nonwhites by force, and he set out to remake the NRA in that image. Under his leadership, the NRA grew from 930,000 members to over 3 million, with an annual budget of $66 million, and became the lobbying juggernaut feared by politicians today. He accomplished this impressive feat with a combination of business savvy and the philosophical fervor of a barnstorming preacher. To attract members, Carter instituted giveaways and discounts—a practice still widely used by the organization to recruit and boost its membership numbers. He adopted a hardline "no compromises" philosophy that presented any effort to make guns harder to get as an infringement on Second Amendment rights.

Carter once told a congressional panel that he would rather allow violent convicted felons, drug addicts, and mentally "deranged" people to buy a gun than require any kind of screening. He described this attitude as "a price we pay for freedom." Carter kept the NRA headquarters in the center of the political action—Washington, DC—and changed the organization's motto from "Firearms Safety Education, Marksmanship Training, Shooting for Recreation" to "The Right of the People to Keep and Bear Arms Shall Not Be Infringed"—a purposely truncated version of the Second Amendment.

Throughout his tenure, the organization prioritized repealing Johnson's Gun Control Act. The law had attracted significant bipartisan support in Congress, but Carter was determined to chip away at it, arguing that it undermined the Second Amendment. He was playing the long game, establishing a bold goal and strategically moving toward it. Twenty years later, the NRA succeeded, at least in part, by winning passage of the Firearm Owners' Protection Act. This act repealed parts of the 1968 law by weakening the authority of the Bureau of Alcohol, Tobacco, Firearms and Explosives (ATF), the federal entity responsible for regulating firearms, to oversee federally licensed gun dealers; it also loosened restrictions on interstate gun sales.

Upon signing the measure, President Ronald Reagan, who as governor of California actually had supported Johnson's law, echoed the NRA's newfound Second Amendment extremism. Six years earlier, he had benefited from the organization's very first presidential endorsement and his reversal on guns typified the evolution of the Republican Party on the issue and highlighted the growing power and influence of the gun lobby.

In 1972 the Republican platform had stated, "We pledge to . . . intensify efforts to prevent criminal access to all weapons, including special emphasis on cheap, readily obtainable handguns, . . . with such federal law as necessary to enable the states to meet their responsibilities." Eight years later, in 1980, the Republican platform said the opposite: "We believe the right of citizens to keep and bear arms must be preserved."

The union between the NRA and the Republican Party was now stronger than ever; its strength lay in its mutual cultural and financial interests. The party's opposition to gun regulations spoke to a growing fundamentalist white rural constituency, but it was particularly important to the industry dedicated to selling more arms.

Gunmakers benefit from the lobby's legislative goals because they can sell more guns to more people. When Carter and his fundamentalists took over the NRA, gunmakers saw an opportunity to use the NRA to advance their interests. The industry has long advertised in NRA magazines and publications, where its products are favorably reviewed, and has stuffed NRA membership forms in product packaging. As the *New York Times* reported back in 1972, "Many firearms manufacturers have chosen to remain in the background of the raging debate over tighter restrictions on the sale and possession of guns, preferring to leave their public talking to the National Rifle Association."[10]

Patriotism, after all, makes for far better rhetoric than messaging about increasing gun sales. In the years that followed, the relationship between the gun lobby, the gun industry, and the Republican Party became a marriage of love as well as convenience.

How the NRA Weaponized the Second Amendment

The NRA began wrapping its marriage to the gun industry in the flag in the 1970s. In that decade, the organization started funding academics to argue that the consensus surrounding the Second Amendment—put forward by Supreme Court decisions, legal scholars, and historians—was faulty. The right to bear arms should not be seen in the context of a militia or as a right of the people to collectively take up firearms for the common defense. According to this revisionist history, the Second Amendment bestowed on *individuals* the right to own and carry firearms wherever they choose. The NRA saw this new interpretation as a way to combat gun restrictions and loosen gun control laws.

Until 1969, the NRA's "individual right" theory existed only on the margins of mainstream opinion. Almost every single academic article on the Second Amendment concluded that it did not guarantee an individual right to own a firearm. But as the NRA began advocating the individual-right theory and investing in it, opinions shifted.

Two decades later, more than half of the scholarly articles on the Second Amendment were arguing that those twenty-seven words protected states' rights to maintain militias *and* the right of any individual to own a firearm. These arguments held that "the people" actually referred to individuals, not the body politic, and that "militia" described able-bodied white men, not an organized military force. Many, if not most, of these opinions were penned by lawyers employed either by the NRA or by similar gun rights organizations; the conflict of interest often went undisclosed. And over time, legal scholars without connections to the gun lobby began to endorse its view as well.[1]

These articles previewed the NRA's messaging in the decades to come. In the early 1990s, the lobby established a nonprofit association of law school professors called Academics for the Second Amendment and launched a Second Amendment essay competition. It provided $1 million to establish the Patrick Henry professorship in constitutional law and the Second Amendment at George Mason University Law School. The organization even paid a lawyer $15,000 to critique historians who rejected the individualist interpretation. The NRA was determined to shift the nation's longstanding understanding and interpretation of our founding document to serve and promote its agenda. It would prove to be a wise investment.

Much of this revisionism came from attorneys, not historians. They plucked a number of quotes from dissenters in the Pennsylvania ratification convention, excerpted from Massachusetts residents who disagreed with the state's constitution, and borrowed other quotes out of context from prominent founding fathers.

For instance, many prominent revisionists and many NRA members cite Patrick Henry's dictum "The great object is, that every man be armed" as proof that the founders believed that individuals should be able to own firearms unrestricted. The remark is even the title of an influential 1984 revisionist history about the Second Amendment. But consult the history or read the quote in its full proper context and you'll learn that far from promoting guns for everyone, Henry was agitating "against the expense of two levels of government—the federal and the state—buying arms for the militia at the same time."[2] The sentence before that infamous quote reads, "At a very great cost, we shall be doubly armed."

Likewise, the NRA and its supporters often pull out a quote by Thomas Jefferson, "One loves to possess arms," as evidence of his love for firearms. But Jefferson was simply requesting old letters he had written, to help him win a political debate. "Tho' I do not know that it will ever be of the least importance to me yet one loves to possess arms tho' they hope never to have occasion for them," Jefferson wrote in full. "They possess my paper in my own handwriting. It is just I should possess theirs. The only thing amiss is that they should have left me to seek a return of the paper, or a copy of it, from you."[3]

Historian Garry Wills sums up the revisionist approach this way: "Time after time, in dreary expectable ways, the quotes bandied about . . . turn out to be truncated, removed from context, twisted, or applied to a debate different from that over the Second Amendment."[4]

Appearing on PBS in 1991, former chief justice Warren Burger, a conservative, used even harsher words than Wills. He described the individual-right theory as "a fraud" and declared that the Second Amendment "has been the subject of one of the greatest pieces of fraud, I repeat the word 'fraud,' on the American public by special interest groups that I have ever seen in my lifetime."

Burger expressed alarm because the NRA's effort was indeed having an impact. By the end of the 1990s, about 67 percent of law review articles about the Second Amendment were adopting the individual-right view and, seventeen years later, it won the day in the Supreme Court. In 2008's *District of Columbia v. Heller*, five justices struck down the Washington, DC, ban on handgun possession and agreed with gun rights advocates that the Constitution guaranteed an individual right to own a firearm in the home for self-defense.

Writing for the majority, Justice Antonin Scalia stressed that that right was not absolute, however, and conceded that the government

can constitutionally ban certain individuals from possessing firearms. It can prohibit the carrying of firearms in schools or government buildings, impose restrictions on their sale, and prohibit
the availability of "particularly dangerous and unusual weapons."
Two years later, in a separate case, the Court ruled that the Second
Amendment applied to states and localities.

In *Heller*, however, the Court reversed decades of legal precedent.
The Supreme Court had previously analyzed the meaning and reach
of the Second Amendment four times and each time had concluded
that it does not extend an individual right to ownership. It did so
most prominently in the 1939 case upholding the constitutionality
of the National Firearms Act. The Court had ruled that the Second
Amendment protected "the right to bear arms" within the context
of a militia and found that the government had the ability to ban
weapons that were unrelated to "some reasonable relationship to the
preservation or efficiency of a well regulated militia." The *Heller*
decision, therefore, represented a legal sea change. While the text
of the amendment didn't change, the new legal and historical arguments put forward by the revisionists provided the Court's conservative justices the justification and pretext they needed to read new
rights into the founding text. Those new rights aligned neatly with
the commercial objectives of the NRA and the political priorities of
the Republican Party.

Multiple factors contributed to the NRA's eventual success. The
lobby helped elect George W. Bush president in 2000. It ensured that
he would appoint to the bench conservative justices who agreed with
the NRA's interpretation of the Second Amendment. Its ability to
shape legal thinking was pivotal, however. On the day the Supreme
Court handed down its decision in *Heller*, Walter Dellinger, who had
represented the District of Columbia in the challenge, told the pro-
gun lawyer who had successfully argued it, "You know, it was the
scholarship that won the case."[5]

But that scholarship and the victory it created did not birth the kind of gun rights renaissance the NRA may have hoped for.

Since *Heller*, and as of this writing, the Supreme Court has been reluctant to accept new challenges to gun-safety laws and has even upheld restrictions on gun rights. The justices turned away at least seventy Second Amendment cases, including: challenges to California's ten-day waiting period to buy a gun, a ban on carrying concealed-carry weapons outside the home, assault weapons bans, and prohibitions against certain classes of individuals from owning firearms. An analysis conducted in 2017 found that "in the more than 1,150 state and federal court decisions" since *Heller*, courts throughout the country "have rejected the Second Amendment challenges 94 percent of the time." Instead, they have upheld numerous gun restrictions, including requiring "good cause" for the issuance of a concealed-carry permit, state laws that prohibit the possession of assault weapons and high-capacity magazines, laws requiring the registration of all firearms and a waiting period before a firearm sale, and state rules that require firearms to meet particular safety standards.[6]

If we know one thing about the NRA, however, it is that as seats are vacated on the high court, the lobby will do everything in its power to install justices who agree with its interpretation and are ready to insert new rights into the Second Amendment, thus loosening gun restrictions even further. The NRA's persistence and singular focus on advancing a "guns everywhere and for everyone" agenda are two keys to its success.

Why the NRA Is Successful

By almost any measure, the NRA is one of the most successful political lobbies the United States has ever seen. Its intense focus on a single issue energizes millions of Americans and transforms their enthusiasm into electoral victories, ensuring that lawmakers on state and federal levels continue to vote down restrictions against gun ownership and advance policies that make firearms more readily available.

Since 1911, the organization has hammered home one clear message: more guns will make you safer. Since the late 1970s, it has insisted that any tightening of gun laws violates the constitutional rights of responsible gun-owning Americans. Despite the lack of evidence for either claim, the lobby has repeated these messages incessantly and thereby transformed American law and public opinion.

On the federal level, the NRA defeated countless efforts to expand background checks to cover all gun sales and to ban military-style assault weapons. It has prevented the government from funding scientific research into gun violence, thwarted efforts by federal regulators to hold gun manufacturers and federally licensed dealers accountable, and even rammed through a federal law protecting both from most forms of liability. The lobby regularly pushes for measures that would allow convicted felons to access guns, opposes measures prohibiting domestic abusers from getting firearms, and advances measures to allow guns at schools, on college campuses, and even in churches and bars.

Conservative lawmakers—practically or literally—copy and paste their firearm policies from the NRA website and regularly consult its lobbyists before weighing in on gun issues. Republican politicians sound no different from NRA lobbyists because they are afraid to cross the organization and confront the wrath of its hardcore base of supporters, as well as millions of other Americans who may not subscribe fully to the organization's political beliefs but see it as an ally that shares their worldview. Combined with the millions of dollars the NRA can throw into an electoral race and its habit of funding the opponents of lawmakers who do cross it, politicians see little incentive to take on the lobby.

Even some progressive lawmakers and advocates fear that too bold a position against guns could energize the NRA and its supporters. As a result, they tamp down their messages and policy proposals to appeal to "responsible" gun owners. That anxiety goes back to the 1994 midterm elections. The NRA energized its followers to vote against twenty-four members of Congress who supported an assault weapons ban and nineteen lost their seats. Twenty-five years later, it remains unclear how much the NRA's campaign contributed to the massive electoral loss for Democrats; the party was also confronting a soft economy and the Clinton administration's unsuccessful effort to reform the health care system. Clinton spoke in favor of gun safety during his 1996 reelection campaign, and in the 2004 election both major-party candidates supported an assault weapons ban. Nevertheless, fear of the NRA dampened enthusiasm for directly confronting the gun issue for decades to come.

On the state level, where nearly all gun policy is made, the lobby's success is even more impressive.

As recently as 1981, nineteen states and the District of Columbia prohibited any form of concealed carry; twenty-nine states allowed officials to use their discretion in granting permits; two states required officials to green-light all applicants not barred by federal law from owning a firearm; just one—Vermont—had a permitless carry system. Today every single state in the union allows individuals to carry concealed weapons outside their homes. At least eight have even enacted permitless carry laws. Individuals who live in Alaska, Arizona, Idaho, Kansas, Maine, Mississippi, Missouri, New Hampshire, North Dakota, Vermont, West Virginia, and Wyoming do not have to meet any requirements for bringing a weapon into a public space.

The NRA also pushed states to adopt constitutional protections for gun owners. As a result, forty-four states now guarantee the individual the right to bear arms.

It lobbied for preemption laws to prevent cities and towns from adopting stricter gun restrictions, arguing that a state should have uniform gun laws throughout. As of 2018, only seven states allow local governments to regulate firearms and ammunition; in forty-three states, local laws about firearms can be preempted by weaker state laws.[1]

Beginning in 2005, the lobby even sought to make it easier for individuals to shoot their guns and claim self-defense. That year, it convinced the Florida legislature and Governor Jeb Bush to sign a so-called stand-your-ground law, which allows individuals to use deadly force in self-defense beyond the home, in any place they have a legal right to be, without fear of prosecution. At least twenty-five states have adopted similar legislation, and the NRA continues to lobby on its behalf. Florida, meanwhile, is experiencing a higher rate of gun violence. Ten years after it enacted stand-your-ground, "justifiable homicides" have increased by 75 percent and one analysis found that "approximately 4,200 individuals were murdered with a gun in Florida whose lives may have been saved if stand your ground had not been enacted and previous trends had continued." For the gun lobby, it is not enough for individuals to have easy access to firearms; they must be able to use them to kill with impunity too.

All of this success on the state level is essential for the NRA's longevity. First, loosening restrictions on gun ownership and making firearms readily available shifts public opinion. In 1999, the year of the Columbine school shooting, 52 percent of Americans believed that gun ownership generally does more to reduce safety than to enhance it. Nineteen years and more than two hundred American school shootings later, 58 percent of respondents to an NBC News and *Wall Street Journal* poll agreed that "gun ownership does more to increase safety by allowing law-abiding citizens to protect themselves." Just 38 percent believed the opposite. The trend flies in the face of countless academic studies that have found that having a gun in the home dramatically increases the chances of homicide, suicide, and accidental shootings.

Second, revising laws on the state level provides gun enthusiasts and supporters more opportunities to take part in the fight; it delivers many more victories for the lobby and its members. It creates a sense of momentum and encourages men and women dedicated to the issue to keep at it.

Third, and most important, state victories affect the development of federal constitutional law. In 2008, when the Supreme Court ruled on *Heller*, it did so against the backdrop of not only NRA-funded research, but also the presence of such individual rights in state constitutions. Ruling in favor of the gun lobby, therefore, allowed the Supreme Court to cause less disruption.

But all of this raises a key question: *why* is the NRA so successful?

The organization has a clear, tight message and a single focus. It distills its pitch into a single word—freedom—and, most importantly, builds a patriotic American identity and community around the emotion that word evokes.

For hardcore members, that identity is rooted in white privilege and anxiety over the changing demographics of America. Others see the NRA and guns generally as representative of an outdoor lifestyle defined by social and cultural bonding activities like hunting and sport shooting. Still others hope to preserve a constitutional principle they believe would be threatened by restrictions on firearms. Some simply want to be able to arm themselves should the need arise.

But even individuals whose relationship with the NRA begins with self-defense are exposed to its political philosophies and social identities. The organization injects its training and safety programs with political ideology and Second Amendment fundamentalism. The gun training course I took had all the trappings of a conservative political convention and the NRA's concealed-carry courses are no different. Jennifer Carlson, who studies American gun culture as assistant professor of sociology and of government and public policy at the University of Arizona, has observed, "Rather than prioritize hands-on defensive training, these courses teach gun carriers that they are a particular kind of person—a law-abiding person willing to use lethal force to protect innocent life."

Whatever their reason for joining the organization, NRA members are also motivated by the threat that they could lose something, and the lobby stokes those fears every chance it gets, framing even the smallest reform as a slippery slope to gun confiscation. Every mass shooting is a chance to warn members that their guns could be taken away and that fear-based messaging breeds loyalty. Polls show that one-fourth of voters who prioritize gun rights have contributed to a gun rights organization, and 45 percent are involved in activism; just 6 percent of gun control supporters have contributed to a gun control group, and only 26 percent have been activists.[2] Another survey found that 71 percent of gun control opponents say they would never support a candidate who wants to restrict gun ownership; only 34 percent of gun control supporters pledged to never back a candidate who does not share their view.

Half of gun owners tell pollsters that owning a firearm is very or somewhat important to their identities. Political scientist Matthew Lacombe argues that this is no accident. He contends that gun owners are politically dedicated to the NRA because it successfully created a social identity related to gun ownership. "Rather than arguing that gun control laws should be opposed because a particular law is flawed in a technical way," Lacombe explains, "the NRA is more likely to say that that gun control provision should be opposed because it represents an attack on who gun owners are and what they stand for." Gun owners, in other words, hold a politically meaningful identity that the NRA constantly depicts as being under threat. Taking political action becomes a means of protecting that identity. Even hunting and target practice are fetishized as political acts that show one's patriotism and macho strength. As one Depression-era *Rifleman* editorial put it, "By your attendance at those regional shoots . . . by your fighting support of your National Association . . . you are showing the nation as you have shown it often in the past that you are its most courageous sons. That from your ranks spring leaders, not followers!" By picking up a firearm, gun owners are not merely taking part in a fun social activity; they are becoming rugged individualists and great American patriots!

The NRA built this identity through its publications and communications with members. Lacombe analyzed seventy-nine years of the NRA's *American Rifleman* magazine and, separately, letters to the editors of four major U.S. newspapers. He wanted to see if gun owners who read the magazine mirrored its arguments in their own public communications.

Lacombe discovered that two-thirds of *Rifleman* editorials portrayed gun rights as being under threat; 80 percent used identity-stroking language that portrayed gun owners in a positive light or described gun regulations and their proponents negatively. The NRA magazine used at least one of the following adjectives to describe gun owners in the majority of its editorials: "law-abiding, peaceable, patriotic, courageous, honest, average citizens, ordinary citizens, brave, freedom-loving, and reputable." Its members consistently echoed the language and internalized the identity.

Of the pro-gun letters to the editor Lacombe analyzed, 64 percent relied on identity language, and almost all used at least one of the honorifics from *Rifleman* editorials. Conversely, the NRA magazine consistently portrayed individuals and institutions it perceives as promoting gun control in a negative light, and the pro-gun letters to the editor echoed that language, too, though at a lower rate. Both the NRA magazine and the pro-gun letter writers have routinely characterized the news media as liars, cowards, and elitists, and gun control proponents as communists, tyrants, and foes of liberty.

"The NRA is able to mobilize large numbers of people in ways that are difficult to do if you just make technical policy-based appeals," Lacombe told me. Seventy-four percent of the NRA's policy editorials framed their arguments in terms of identity. Fifty-four percent of pro-gun editorial writers did the same, focusing on how the proposed policy would affect the lives of gun owners. Gun control advocates, on the other hand, focused their editorials on projections of crime reduction and rarely used personal terms, a losing strategy as facts mean less and less to more and more people.

The lobby uses the same language and techniques today.

In 2018, the NRA's top priority was concealed-carry reciprocity, which if enacted into law would require every state in the nation to allow concealed carry within its borders—even if the carriers have no training. It is seeking to make silencers readily available to gun owners and is pushing more states to allow permitless carry.

In laying out this agenda to members on the NRA website, chief lobbyist Chris Cox spends multiple paragraphs describing gun owners as "law-abiding Americans" and reminding them of the role firearms play in their lives. "Hunting contributes to the sound management of natural resources, strengthens ties within families and between friends, and instills a love of nature and the outdoors," he writes. "The shooting sports build character, awareness, and the competency necessary for responsible gun ownership."[3]

Even the policies themselves are framed in personal terms. Concealed-carry reciprocity would allow a "mild-mannered tailor or grocer" to carry a concealed weapon in public. Making silencers readily available "protects the health of shooters and results in a substantially better shooting experience." The article lacks any statistics or policy analysis; it simply panders to the members' social identities as responsible gun owners.[4]

As former NRA president David Keene explained, "The difference between the NRA and other groups is that we've developed a community [and] when they see Second Amendment rights threatened they vote. They do whatever they need to do."

How the NRA Channels Hatred into Political Success

In its appeals to gun owners' social identity, the NRA exploits people's fears about the country's changing demographics. Thus it openly courts extremists to advance its agenda and engage its followers. The most visible manifestation of this approach began in the 1990s, as the NRA orchestrated increasingly harsh rhetorical attacks against the Clinton administration's laws instituting background checks and banning assault weapons.

Jim Brady, a former press secretary to Ronald Reagan, was paralyzed when a would-be assassin's bullet intended for the president struck him in the head instead. In 1993, he helped secure passage of the Brady Handgun Violence Prevention Act. The law required background checks for anyone who purchased a firearm from federally licensed gun dealers. It's still the foundation of the background-check system. The NRA argued that the law was "the first step" toward gun confiscation and immediately challenged its constitutionality in court. It suffered another defeat a year later, when it failed to prevent passage of a measure outlawing military-style assault weapons for civilian use.

The lobby responded to the losses by courting extremists. As one former NRA board member told the *Boston Globe* in 1995, the NRA launched a campaign to openly recruit antigovernment activists and began sending members fund-raising emails and writing articles claiming that the government was coming for their guns and possibly even their lives. The NRA figured the fringe movement could help build its membership, increase revenue, and generate more foot soldiers for the coming political fights. It proved to be a dangerous gamble.

During this period, the NRA started recruiting at gun shows attended by antigovernment militia members, giving away free hats, and publicizing their events in the *Rifleman*. Sister publications featured militia members in cover stories and profiles. NRA leaders openly compared FBI agents to Nazis, claiming that Clinton's ban on assault weapons gave "jack-booted government thugs more power to take away our Constitutional rights, break in our doors, seize our guns, destroy our property and even injure or kill us." Tanya Metaksa, then the executive director of the NRA's lobbying army, even called for and attended a meeting with two leaders of the largest and best-organized antigovernment groups. As militia commander Ken Adams later described it, Metaksa was hoping to "formalize how we would work together."

That meeting took place just two months before Timothy McVeigh, who had been an NRA member for at least four years, carried out his bomb attack in Oklahoma City. The Alfred P. Murrah Federal Building housed an office of the agency responsible for overseeing the gun industry. Three years earlier, McVeigh had sent a letter to Congress that read like an NRA manifesto. "I strongly believe in a God-given right to self defense," he wrote. "Should any other person or a governing body be able to tell another person that he/she cannot save their own life?" Attached to the back of that envelope was a decal that read, "I'm the NRA."

In validating and amplifying the antigovernment message of the fringe and actively recruiting from within it, the NRA gambled that nobody would act on its rhetoric. After McVeigh did, killing 168 people in the worst act of terror by an American in America, the organization came under fire.

President George H.W. Bush resigned from the organization in protest, and articles began popping up drawing connections between the terror in Oklahoma and the NRA's mailings and recruitment efforts.

The *New York Times* editorialized in May of 1995, "With his ferocious resignation letter, Mr. Bush dealt a disabling blow to the N.R.A.'s prestige and to Mr. LaPierre's standing as a public figure. . . . It now looks as if his action will become a watershed moment in the N.R.A.'s history and deprive it of its last claims to respectability. The outfit is reeling."[1]

Only when he felt forced to do so did NRA president Wayne LaPierre offer a rare apology for the "jack-booted government thugs" fund-raising letter. Metaksa repeatedly denied that she had courted militia members, even though multiple NRA board members with strong ties to the "patriot movement" remained on the board.

The outfit was, in fact, in trouble. It needed a reboot, a more media-friendly face to stop the bleeding and hold back the backlash. It had just the man for the job: Moses.

Charlton Heston was an Oscar-winning actor who had appeared in blockbuster films, including *The Ten Commandments* and *Planet of the Apes*. Once a supporter of the civil rights movement and the Gun Control Act of 1968, Heston, by the 1980s, had associated himself with the conservative social politics of Ronald Reagan. In the eyes of the NRA, he was the perfect man to put a holy face on the lobby's extremist rhetoric.

Everything became culture war as the NRA saddled up to the reactionary religious right. The war pitted, and still pits, privileged straight white men like Heston against everyone else. Gay men, lesbians, feminists, African Americans, Native Americans, Asian Americans, Latin American Americans, communists, liberals, atheists, progressives of every stripe, and the media were on one side. "Manly" white men, their women, and their allegedly Christian family values were on the other.

A year before he assumed the helm of the organization, Heston previewed this approach in a speech delivered to a conservative think tank. Its dog-whistle invocations of racism, homophobia, and good-ol'-boy white male supremacy were topped with a steaming pile of fear. After comparing the plight of straight white conservative men in America to that of Jews in the Third Reich, Heston cataloged the many ways "true" Americans are "oppressed":

> The gun issue clearly brings into focus the war that's going on. . . .
>
> Heaven help the God-fearing, law-abiding, Caucasian, middle-class, Protestant, or—even worse—Evangelical Christian, Midwest, or Southern, or—even worse—rural, apparently straight, or—even worse—admittedly heterosexual, gun-owning, or—even worse—NRA-card-carrying, average working stiff, or—even worse—male working stiff, because not only don't you count, you're a downright obstacle to social progress. Your tax dollars may be just as delightfully green as you hand them over, but your voice requires a lower decibel level, your opinion is less enlightened, your media access is insignificant, and frankly, mister, you need to wake up, wise up, and learn a little something about your new America, and until you do, would you mind shutting up?
>
> Mainstream America is depending on you—counting on you—to draw your sword and fight for them. These people have precious little time or resources to battle misguided Cinderella attitudes, the fringe propaganda of

the homosexual coalition, the feminists who preach that
it's a divine duty for women to hate men, blacks who raise
a militant fist with one hand while they seek preference
with the other, and all the New-Age apologists for juve-
nile crime, who see roving gangs as a means of youthful
expression, sex as a means of adolescent merchandizing,
violence as a form of entertainment for impressionable
minds, and gun bans as a means to lord-knows-what.
We have reached that point in time when our national
social policy originates on *Oprah*. I say it's time to pull
the plug.[2]

Sound familiar? It should. The NRA still heaps praise on
Heston—who remained with the organization until 2003—and it
eagerly uses his strategy of pandering to the insecurities of white
men by casting them as victims.

In 2004, the NRA launched an entire network, NRATV, dedicated to doing just that. Turn it on and you will hear how Mus-
lim, black, brown, gay, lesbian, bisexual, transgender, feminist, and
Democratic people are undermining America's culture and constitutional liberties.

President Barack Obama is a "demographically symbolic president," LaPierre told NRA members. Black Lives Matter focuses too
much on police brutality, they say. After all, "90 percent or more
of the racial problems that we have in this country are manufactured by the left," a host on NRATV has said. Trans women are just
"pretending" to be women. "All radicalized terrorists are Muslims."
The list goes on and on.

Throughout the Obama years, the NRA sent out countless dire
warnings about our nation's first black president confiscating firearms. Those warnings pushed millions to buy more firearms and
filled the NRA coffers with donations.

In a December 2009 direct-mail letter, LaPierre warned of "massive armies of anti-gun, anti-freedom radicals marshaling against us for an attack that could make every other battle we've ever fought look like a walk in the park. . . . And I can guarantee you that in this 'new' America—an America unlike anything you can even imagine—your firearms and your Second Amendment rights WON'T be welcome."

Such messages are still the norm, and militaristic calls to violence are still part of the strategy. The following piece of direct mail is not much different from the kind of rhetoric you would expect to find in ISIS recruitment materials. Here, the NRA urges members to "sacrifice" themselves in the name of firearm freedom. "Our Constitution and our system of government guarantee that every American has the opportunity to write his or her name in the history books of tomorrow—to leave his or her imprint on the fabric of our nation. But in the end, history is always written only by a select few—the few who sacrifice of themselves to fight for the causes in which they believe."[3]

For the Trump era, the lobby and its properties have transformed themselves into the kind of state media you found in my former and no longer existent home country, the Soviet Union. The NRA defends Trump at every turn and viciously attacks the mainstream media for accurately reporting on his administration. It is the ultimate us-versus-them dynamic. "The only way we save our country and our freedom is to fight this violence of lies with the clenched fist of truth," spokesperson Dana Loesch told NRA members in one popular video, her eyes sternly and seriously staring into the camera. "I'm the National Rifle Association, and I'm freedom's safest place." These videos feature an absurd number of black-and-white images to visually communicate how the country is falling apart, its traditions and values under attack. Loesch threatens to burn copies of the *New York Times* and attacks other popular newspapers, pretending that they lie about freedom-loving NRA members; she shows fast images of landmarks in Washington, DC, and other cities, implying that they're full of people intent on destroying all things American, beginning with the Second Amendment.[4]

The NRA reinforces the anxieties of a no longer all-powerful conservative minority in a way that interweaves conservative social intolerance with the politics of gun rights. The latter is at times indistinguishable from the former. In 2018, it is hitching itself to a particular president and his constituency, possibly alienating gun owners who do not subscribe to the president's racism, sexism, and authoritarianism. Thus it risks losing power once the political winds change. Some gun owners are already objecting.

We Know How to Reduce Gun Violence

One Friday evening in September 2016, just two days before the three-month anniversary of the devastating shooting at the Pulse nightclub in Orlando, Florida, I took a deep breath and opened up the Skype application on my laptop. I had scheduled an interview with Chris Hansen, a bearish gay man in his early thirties who had survived that tragedy. He had agreed to film a video for Guns Down America, the very first we would produce as an organization.

As I began testing my camera, I thought of how I first learned of the shooting on the summer Sunday morning of June 12, 2016. I had woken up from a night at a not-so-different dance club in Washington, DC, the city where I had lived for the past eight years. The night began at a friend's LGBT Pride house party—held every year in a narrow row house overflowing with people pre-gaming for the festivities ahead: a parade down DC's main stretch and then a night of partying at one of the many bars in the District. The place was overflowing with Jello shots, keg stands, loud music, and a particularly memorable young gay man wearing a rainbow flag as a cape. He was cheerfully giving hugs and shots to everyone he came across; he embodied the happiness and joy of someone who was experiencing his very first Pride celebration. It was a festive atmosphere, one of those parties that made you forget the anxieties and stresses of daily life and allowed you to just live and celebrate the moment.

Pride has always felt magical in the District. The holiday is a citywide celebration that unites, in a very real and moving way, the city's LGBT and straight communities. This particular party, for instance, was hosted by a straight woman who invited a mix of her gay and straight friends; the parade that followed the party featured chiseled gay men standing alongside gay and lesbian families with children, and straight families with children, all cheering, applauding, and jumping for beads from the floats representing local government, businesses, and advocacy organizations.

Eight hundred fifty miles away, Chris and his fellow Pride revelers were likely taking part in a very similar celebration and feeling the same warmth, inclusion, and acceptance that many of us in the LGBT community struggle to find, and hold tightly to once we do.

That is, they *were*, until a gunman walked into that party with a Sig Sauer MCX rifle, a weapon originally designed for U.S. Special Operations forces, and opened fire.

The first alert I read as I woke up that morning placed the number of people killed at twenty-four, but it was clear from the report that the casualty count would climb higher. I scrolled further through the alerts and found several messages sent to me from some of my followers on Twitter highlighting examples of lawmakers already sending their "thoughts and prayers." Another familiar cycle had begun.

Through the incredibly numbing pain of the tragedy, the anger that animated me and many others that day was directed at elected officials whom we trust to secure our families and protect our communities. Unfortunately, too many of them focus on protecting their own political longevity, ignoring the needs of the people they represent. These politicians advance their careers and grow their own prestige and power by hitching their train to the gun industry and the NRA. Their empty thoughts and insincere prayers are nothing more than an empathy veneer, covering up their selfish political calculations and impulses and, to some degree, convincing themselves of their essential goodness and humanity. Even after tweeting out the same canned "thoughts and prayers" messages four or five times a year, many elected officials do not seem to realize that thoughts and prayers have failed to stop mass shooters.

Three months later, when I spoke to Chris, I learned just how gruesome that experience had been.

Chris had gone to Pulse nightclub for the very first time on June 12, 2016, to meet someone he had been talking to online. He had just moved to Orlando from Ohio—packed up his car and drove halfway across the country. Chris was eager to meet new people, dance, party, and have a good time. In Pulse, he sought out a spot where he could let loose and be himself. The night took a turn for the worse almost from the very beginning. The guy he was meeting showed up, but then left a half hour later, telling Chris that the club just wasn't up to his standards and that he had a headache. It was an uncomfortable and negative interaction, leaving Chris with a bad taste in his mouth and regret for agreeing to meet the guy in the first place. But he liked the club. "The vibe was nice and people looked like they were having fun." He stayed, had a couple of drinks, and started grooving to the music.

"Before the shooting started, I remember standing up against the wall with a drink in my hand that I had just ordered from the bar. Suddenly, I heard the first shots coming from my left. Because I was leaning against the wall and I could feel the vibrations from my feet and I was like wow, the bass is really kicking on this new song," he recalled.

Pop, pop, pop. Te, te, te, te, te.

The sounds resembled a thumping beat, suddenly accompanied by a flashing light. Chris first confused the flash with a strobe light, not an uncommon feature in a nightclub. Then screaming started. Glasses began to shatter at the bar and fall to the floor. The person standing against the wall next to Chris suddenly fell and he too instinctively crouched down and began to crawl toward the back exit, past the commotion of yelling, screaming, and flying blood. He wasn't quite sure what was happening, but something inside him told him to just keep moving, to keep crawling toward the light that had appeared when the back door of the club was flung open by other people desperately trying to get out. While on the floor, Chris noticed a big red stain on his arm. He thought it was a spilled drink. He smeared it and realized it was someone's blood. He kept crawling.

"I just got all the way out to the door and the back patio, I felt the cement on my arms, I knew I was outside." He got up and ran toward the fence that a group of club goers had already knocked over. Everyone around him was screaming and yelling, running in all directions. Chris darted to the right, sprinting through parking lots and streets before ending up between two palm trees with other survivors. It was only then that he realized what was happening.

The noises and the shots and the screaming were real. The blood was real too. Dozens of people had been hurt by a light that wasn't a strobe light at all, but an assault weapon in the hands of a murderer determined to kill as many people as possible. As he heard the sirens in the distance, he ran back in the direction of the shooting. "I wasn't hurt, so I did the only thing I knew I could do, and that was to help people, carry people, move people, wrap people," he told me. "In a split second you realize you have to do something."

As he saw a man who was shot being carried out of Pulse by his friend, Chris jumped under the injured man's other arm and helped carry him onto the sidewalk. When the injured man didn't have the strength to go farther, Chris took his bandana off his head and shoved it into a bullet wound to help stop the bleeding. He kept pressure on that wound until an emergency responder appeared with a board to carry him away. Amid the chaos, Chris continued down the sidewalk and saw a young woman who had been shot in the arm and in the back. Along with another man, they laid her head in Chris's lap and her back on his legs. As others rushed to flag down one of the paramedics with the boards, Chris kept her awake and focused by asking where she was from, her name, and date of birth. "She was only nineteen," he said. He does not know what happened to her. He hasn't seen her since. "It would be nice to meet her again. It is really challenging to have the not-knowing. To still have the not-knowing," he told me.

Chris, like many survivors of mass tragedies, wonders why he was spared. He's going to church more, reading the Bible, looking for answers. He's struggling with nightmares, noises, flickering of the light. He keeps his cell phone on silent so that it doesn't startle him. He's proud of how he handled himself that night. "If I went down, I would know that it was for a purpose and it wasn't because I was a coward; it was because I was courageous," he told me.

The day after the tragedy, his dad took to Facebook to express how much he admired his son's brave actions. "I am so proud of my son. Both as a man, and as a gay man," Chris's father, Bill, wrote. "He helped so many people. I saw him on the news on Fox and CNN this morning. My son! A hero! Amongst all of the tragedy, helping others." If you're crying while you're reading that, I did too. Gun violence is filled with so much tragedy, sadness, and anger that the expressions of love amid it are especially significant and touching.

Since the shooting, Chris had been to another nightclub on just two other occasions. He enjoyed the people he was with, "but the feeling I had inside was not something I really want to feel," he said. "That fear is going to always be there when you walk into that dark room with the music and the lights and the excitement and see how everybody is enjoying themselves. But then you have that feeling of: Is it the last? Is it the last? Is it the last? And I can't have that feeling anymore."

As I listened and watched Chris tell me his story over Skype, I wondered how the incident had affected his views on firearms. After all, he hails from a gun-owning family that often hunted for dinner. Chris's father, Bill, hadn't even bought meat from a supermarket until he started college, and Chris owned several shotguns growing up.

"We need to have better training," he told me. "If you own a weapon, you should know how to use a weapon and not in the wrong way. There has to be a reason to have a gun," he said.

His answer was simple, eloquent common sense. It also caught me off guard. Politicians in Washington—even those who strongly advocate gun-safety reforms—twist themselves into pretzels to assume positions that they think will be both acceptable to their constituents and politically possible. They talk about solutions that they believe could make it through the convoluted and often unpredictable political process—background checks, closing the terror-list gap—as opposed to the very best solutions to reduce gun deaths, solutions so simple that they often have to come to Washington from people like Chris instead of lawmakers.

If you need a license to drive a car, why not have a license to obtain a firearm? If you have to pass a road test to get that license, shouldn't you be required to undergo field and safety training to demonstrate that you actually know how to use and properly store and keep your firearms? Shouldn't the government know how many deadly weapons its citizens own?

Simple. Easy. Common sense. Lawmakers and advocates on either side never make the case for these straightforward national reforms anymore.

They used to: Lyndon Johnson passionately argued for national licensing and firearm registration after Bobby Kennedy was gunned down in 1968. In 1969, Johnson established the National Commission on the Causes and Prevention of Violence, just as firearms were killing eight thousand people each year. The body called for bold reform: "Our studies have convinced us that the heart of any effective national firearms policy for the United States must be to reduce the availability of the firearm that contributes the most to violence. This means restrictive licensing of the handgun." It urged the government to establish federal standards for gun ownership under which individuals would have to demonstrate need before acquiring firearms.

Congress, beholden to the gun lobby, has buried policies designed to make it harder for people to obtain firearms, arguing that the Constitution's Second Amendment prohibits such reforms, even though they have successfully reduced gun deaths in many other countries all around the world.

The New Second Amendment Compact

Americans are sick and tired of a system that fosters senseless mass shootings, everyday gun violence, gun suicides, and accidental gun deaths. We as a country are ready to embrace the following New Second Amendment Compact and its goal of building a future with fewer guns. The New Second Amendment Compact has three key objectives: regulating the gun industry, making guns significantly harder to get, and investing in communities most impacted by gun violence. The goal is to build a future with significantly fewer guns and thus fewer gun crimes, gun accidents, and gun suicides. The Compact recognizes that the Second Amendment of the U.S. Constitution protects the right to bear arms but that it also empowers citizens and their governments to regulate that right and prioritize community safety.

The Compact has ten simple elements.

1. End gun manufacturer immunity from civil lawsuits and criminal prosecution.
2. Increase oversight and regulation of gun manufacturers.
3. Regulate gun dealers.
4. Prohibit the sale of semiautomatic weapons and high-capacity magazines to civilians.
5. Provide incentives for people to give up their existing firearms.

6. Make licensing and firearm registration mandatory.
7. Require all gun owners to have insurance, à la car insurance.
8. End open carry.
9. Fund scientific research to identify the best ways to reduce gun violence.
10. Invest in community-based programs to do so.

The recipe for significantly lowering gun violence is no mystery. The cause of our national disgrace is easy access to firearms. *Guns* are the problem. Researchers have consistently found that, once you limit gun availability and create an environment where guns are significantly harder to get, gun deaths—homicides, suicides, and mass shootings—drop.

Researchers from the Harvard School of Public Health concluded that "in homes, cities, states and regions in the U.S., where there are more guns, both men and women are at a higher risk for homicide, particularly firearm homicide." Even after the scientists controlled for factors like poverty and urbanization, "for every age group, people in states with many guns" are more likely to be murdered with those guns. They are also more likely to kill themselves or accidentally discharge them.[1] A 2013 study even estimated that for every percentage-point increase in gun ownership, the homicide rate increases by 0.9 percent.[2]

A growing body of research has identified a correlation between strong gun laws and lower rates of gun violence. "The 10 states with the weakest gun laws collectively have an aggregate level of gun violence that is 3.2 times higher than the 10 states with the strongest gun laws," a 2016 report from the Center for American Progress concluded. This means that in states where firearms are significantly harder to get, fewer people die from firearm suicides, homicides, and accidental firearm fatalities. An analysis released by researchers at Harvard University in October of 2018 even found that "a fatal police shooting was 40 percent more likely to happen in states with more guns." No matter how you slice it, it seems, more guns result in more gun deaths.

Areas with higher levels of gun ownership also experience more deaths of law enforcement officers. Researchers discovered that differences in the number of police assassinated "are best explained not by differences in crime, but by differences in household gun ownership." Law enforcement officials are three times more likely to be murdered in a state with one of the highest rates of gun ownership than in one of the states where people own the fewest guns per capita.

Gun enthusiasts typically respond to such facts with a seemingly commonsense slogan: the only thing that can stop a bad guy with a gun is a good guy with a gun. The solution, they say, is to let responsible armed individuals protect their communities, particularly if they live in high-crime areas or in rural locations where police are slow to respond.

Few data exist to support this argument. While armed bystanders have interfered in certain instances and helped mitigate the damage, on the whole, untrained gun owners are rarely equipped to deal with emergency situations and sometimes even do more harm than good. An FBI study of 160 incidents between 2000 and 2013 found that twenty-one active shooters were stopped by unarmed civilians, while just one was stopped by someone carrying a firearm.[3] Moreover, a slew of research has found that concealed-carry permit holders—who insert more guns into our public spaces—actually increase the incidence of violent crime by turning disputes or disagreements into deadly confrontations. George Zimmerman's murder of Trayvon Martin is just the most prominent recent example. Even armed police officers have a hard time reacting to mass shooting in which the perpetrator is firing a military-style assault weapon. The armed officer at the Pulse nightclub, for instance, could not prevent the tragic life loss, and a study of thirty-three mass public shootings from 2009 to 2014 found that over half occurred in areas where people could carry concealed firearms or security guards were present.[4]

Moving the country toward a future with fewer guns will require a multi-pronged approach. Under the terms of this Compact, the federal government would tightly regulate the gun industry and licensed gun dealers, restricting the production and sale of the deadliest guns and ammunition. First on the chopping block would be semiautomatic assault weapons and high-capacity magazines, which are designed to kill as many people as possible as efficiently as possible. That kind of equipment should be only for military use and must not be in the hands of civilians. As Justice Scalia put it, "The right secured by the Second Amendment is not unlimited" and "commentators and courts routinely explained that the right [secured by the Second Amendment] was not a right to keep and carry any weapon whatsoever in any manner whatsoever and for whatever purpose." The assault weapon, therefore, is a firearm that can be constitutionally outlawed.

The Compact would require the federal government to work with private and state partners to fund a national gun buyback program that gives people incentives to sell their handguns and rifles. Gun owners who choose not to would have to register the firearms they hold on to and obtain a federal gun-ownership license from local law enforcement officials. They would be restricted from transferring their existing guns or selling them to persons who do not themselves possess a proper license.

Americans who want to buy firearms would be able to do so but would have to meet tough minimum standards to prove that they know how to safely use and store a gun. Furthermore, they would have to take out liability insurance on that firearm, wait ten days to receive the gun, and demonstrate knowledge of all applicable laws.

The proposals in this Compact seem bold today but are squarely in line with the constitutional precedent established by the Supreme Court. They are true commonsense reforms that an overwhelming majority of Americans already support. They are policies that have reduced gun violence almost everywhere else in the world. If implemented properly and justly, they will dig us, too, out of the gun-violence crisis we have created.

We Must Not Overcriminalize
Gun Owners

The Compact aims to reduce the number of guns in circulation and ensure that individuals who do own them know how to use them safely. In working to achieve this goal, the United States must not overcriminalize gun owners, and we must not build a future with fewer guns on the backs of those who are harmed most by the gun crisis. The Compact must not contribute to or perpetuate inequalities and injustices in our mass-incarceration criminal justice system, in which the prison population has quintupled since the 1970s and 60 percent of prisoners are people of color.

That is why the very first provisions of the Compact, outlined in detail below, go after the big fish in the gun supply chain, the gunmakers and dealers who produce and sell these deadly products. In 2017, the gun industry claimed it produced $51 billion in economic activity. It has grown mightily as a result of the nation's loose gun laws; any effort to build a future with fewer guns must start at the very top and provide significant oversight of the industry and its products.

Any such effort must also deal with the everyday gun violence that plagues our cities. As I have noted, most urban gun homicides occur in clusters of very densely populated and impoverished communities in which people have few economic opportunities and must rely on black markets, primarily created by the drug war, to survive. In such a milieu, guns mean personal protection and become a basic necessity. If we ask people to put down their guns, we have to give them something they can pick up—jobs, job training, scholarships, public works programs, addiction treatment instead of prison . . . there are many possibilities for helping people out of the mess that four centuries of institutionalized racism and exploitation have created.

We must intervene in the cycle of gun violence *without* arresting more people and sending them to prison, for that will dig low-income communities both rural and urban into a deeper financial hole, taking away the few economic opportunities they have and giving them nothing in return. Cities throughout the country have launched community-based crime intervention initiatives that have reduced gun homicide rates. We must pair investments in these programs with policies that will make guns scarce and make new firearms significantly harder to get.

To move toward a world with fewer guns, we need new rules. These rules must limit the possibility that existing firearms will be used in homicides or suicides and restrict the purchase of new firearms. Some current gun owners will face penalties for owning a weapon without a license, insurance, or registration. All of these penalties must be enforced equitably; they cannot be used by politicians and law enforcement as yet another excuse to overcriminalize communities of color. These penalties cannot be the harsh mandatory minimums that have ripped apart communities. We should not be putting people in jail for years for this. Illegal gun possession should be treated as a serious crime to help deter people from committing it, but we cannot continue to overcriminalize the poor or communities of color.

How can we accomplish these objectives fairly? One model to follow could be the successful Swift, Certain, and Fair program widely used for drug and alcohol offenses in Hawaii and elsewhere. SCF replaces long incarceration periods with swift, certain, and relatively small penalties. It is based on the theory that some offenders do not need to spend years in a prison to understand the consequences of their crimes.

Consider individuals on drug probation. Those who test positive for illegal drugs are immediately given a sentence of a couple of days in prison rather than languishing in the criminal justice system or awaiting a court date. It is no longer a question of whether you will end up in jail after you exhaust all of your appeals, but instead it is a certainty that you will go to jail tomorrow. The sentence must be seen as reasonable by the offender in order to change behavior. When it is, it appears that it can. According to a five-year study conducted by the Department of Justice, compared to people in regular probation, individuals in Hawaii's program were 50 percent less likely to be arrested or have their probation revoked and were a whopping 72 percent less likely to use illegal drugs. Length of sentences for gun crimes still varies based on the individual and the community, but this kind of swift approach should be a starting point for designing the penalties for carrying a gun without a license or proper registration.

Another way to avoid contributing to the ills of our criminal justice system is to ensure that the reforms outlined in the Compact are implemented nationally and do not target certain regions or neighborhoods. National implementation will eliminate the problem of guns seeping into communities from less regulated states or jurisdictions. (Approximately 60 percent of guns used in crimes in Chicago come from outside the state.) It will also ensure that gun laws do not have a disparate impact on underserved communities.

The reforms in the Compact are absolutely essential to building safer communities. They have already succeeded in reducing gun deaths around the world—all without infringing on one's right to own guns *responsibly*.

End Gun Manufacturer Immunity

Companies that produce products specifically designed to kill people require thoughtful and responsible oversight. That's just common sense. The government has a public interest in ensuring that the products gun manufacturers produce are marketed and used as safely as possible. If gun manufacturers are reckless and lawmakers fail to hold them accountable, they should both have to answer for their behavior under laws against public endangerment.

Currently, the gun industry exploits loopholes and weak laws to maximize profits. Worse, it is protected from legal liability by a federal law called the Protection of Lawful Commerce in Arms Act (PLCAA). The NRA has also successfully lobbied thirty-four states to provide similar legal immunity within their own jurisdictions. All of these laws shield gun manufacturers and dealers from facing lawsuits when they sell their inherently dangerous products in dangerous ways.

PLCAA came out of a slew of legal challenges in the 1990s and the early 2000s that culminated in an effort to sue gunmakers for continuing to knowingly sell guns to dealers who regularly funneled weapons to criminals and for failing to include safety features that could have saved lives. In 2000, Smith & Wesson settled several of these civil lawsuits and agreed to sell safety devices with its handguns and hold its authorized dealers to a certain code of conduct.

Four years later, Bushmaster agreed to alter its distribution practices after families of the victims killed by the DC Snipers sued the manufacturer and Bull's Eye Shooter Supply for negligent sales practices. A study of the effects of undercover police stings and civil lawsuits on gun dealers concluded that these techniques significantly reduced their willingness to sell guns to criminals.[1]

But the lawsuits posed a real financial threat to the gun industry. Manufacturers feared that they would have to pass the costs of large jury awards on to consumers, pricing some buyers out of the marketplace and perhaps forcing smaller gunmakers out of business. Therefore, in 2005, the NRA successfully lobbied Congress to pass—and President George W. Bush to sign—a law that prevents victims or surviving relatives from suing a gun manufacturer or dealer when the shooting is negligent or criminal. Few other industries enjoy such protection.

Consumers, for instance, can sue General Motors if it makes cars that can't withstand a minor crash. The person who crashes the car is partly responsible for the accident—she may be driving recklessly or under the influence—but we as a society have agreed that General Motors is liable for producing steering wheels that hurt drivers when they get into collisions or developing brakes that don't work properly in stress situations. Manufacturers of a product must prepare for the worst, for reality, not for best-case scenarios. Gun manufacturers and gun dealers pushed through a law to exempt them from this very basic principle that defines the relationship between corporations and governmental oversight. Under this law, gunmakers cannot be held liable for marketing firearms in a way that feeds an illegal market and allows those guns to be used by criminal syndicates, nor can they be sued for failing to implement safety features that could make firearms safer.

When a thirteen-year-old boy pulled the trigger of his father's handgun because he believed it was unloaded and unintentionally killed his thirteen-year-old friend, the Illinois Supreme Court dismissed the family's lawsuit against the gunmaker, Beretta. The court found that the boy acted as a criminal in a negligent way and absolved the manufacturer from any potential liability. The family claimed that Beretta could have easily prevented the tragedy if it had included additional features like an internal lock, a magazine-disconnect safety, or a chamber-loaded indicator. But the case was never considered on its merits. The company faced no pressure—financial or otherwise—to manufacture safer guns. The family was prohibited from accessing the court system to seek relief.

Similarly, relatives of victims from the shooting at Sandy Hook Elementary School in Newtown, Connecticut, filed a lawsuit against Remington, the manufacturer of the military-style assault rifle that killed twenty-six people on December 14, 2012. The suit claimed that the company should be held responsible for marketing to untrained civilians a firearm designed to kill as many people as possible as fast as possible. The lawsuit also argued that the marketing materials for Remington's AR-15-style Bushmaster specifically targeted young men and appealed to them with hypermasculine and violent messaging. An ad for the gun included the tagline, "Consider your man card reissued."

Nevertheless, a judge dismissed the lawsuit from the Connecticut Superior Court, citing the gun industry's immunity. "This action falls squarely within the broad immunity provided," she said.[2]

Increase Oversight and Regulation of Gun Manufacturers

Before bringing a product to market, manufacturers must contract with a federally certified laboratory to test its product for safety. The laboratory will ensure that the product doesn't pose an electrical or mechanical hazard and guarantee that the packaging is safe and that the product itself doesn't include toxic metals and can be used safely by customers. Once the laboratory has completed its work, the manufacturer can then certify that, based on the test results, the product complies with all mandated safety rules.

Consumer advocates have long applauded these guidelines, arguing that they have prevented numerous injuries and saved countless lives.

But the description above applies to toy manufacturers, not gunmakers. In fact, cars, toys, and aspirin all have to meet mandatory safety standards. Guns do not. Many guns made in America do not go through safety testing to ensure they include the most basic safety features.[1] No federal agency oversees how firearms are designed or built. Just seven states and the District of Columbia have enacted laws to address federally unregulated domestic junk guns. California, Massachusetts, and New York have the most comprehensive design and safety standards for handguns. Why does this matter? An October 2012 study from the Johns Hopkins Center for Gun Policy Research found that improved safety standards might prevent many unintentional, accidental shootings, which killed 4,000 Americans and injured over 95,000 between 2005 and 2010.

Highlighting a particularly egregious example of gun manufacturer negligence, a CNBC investigation in 2010 found that for decades Remington Arms secretly considered recalling its rifles due to a design flaw. Customers bought rifles that would discharge even if no one pulled the trigger; twenty-four people died and one hundred were injured as a result. Remington finally redesigned its trigger in 2007, but with no federal oversight, it was able to resist doing this for years and keep the claims under wraps.[2]

Gunmakers do not have to reveal exactly what they manufacture, in what quantities they manufacture it, or how they distribute their products. This lack of information makes it harder—almost impossible—for policy makers to understand the industry, count the number of guns in circulation, and identify where they are.

We should not be relying on an honor system in which gun manufacturers can simply police themselves. Firearm makers must be required to meet tough new transparency standards in reporting what products they manufacture, how many firearms they make every single year, and where those products are distributed. They should also be required to serialize additional parts of the gun and shell casings to allow law enforcement agencies to easily identify the weapon if it is used to commit a crime. Currently, only the frame or receiver must be marked, making it easy to file off the number. Many foreign manufacturers serialize other components, like barrels and magazines, but U.S. manufacturers do only what is required and no more. We as Americans deserve better.

The gun industry should be required to meet stiff safety standards and be subject to oversight by the Consumer Product Safety Commission, just like the toys I described above. The CPSC protects the public from unsafe and dangerous products through public safety warnings and recalls and it must expand its mandate to include guns.

Firearms were left out of its purview by former Michigan representative John Dingell. His wife, Representative Debbie Dingell, who
now holds his seat, has since introduced a bill in Congress to include
firearms in the commission's mandate.

The truth is, such oversight is more important now than ever
before. Firearm manufacturers, in an effort to improve market
share, are producing new products and militarized firearm acces
sories that may actually be making guns more dangerous. These
changes are designed to excite an already saturated customer base as
gun ownership rates are shrinking and the gun supply is increasingly
concentrated in the hands of fewer people.

The industry is producing devices that mimic fully automatic fire;
AR and AK pistols, which are guns that mimic short-barreled rifles;
and pistol stabilizing braces, which are being used to function as a
shoulder stock, transforming the pistol into a short-barreled rifle,
a weapon currently restricted under federal law. Since these pistols
fire rifle calibers, their rounds travel three times faster than pistol
rounds, penetrate common police body armor, and create devastating wounds. These new firearms and accessories are making crime
more deadly. In Chicago, researchers have noticed that the average
weapon caliber used in everyday gun violence has been going up
and that the number of people killed with high-velocity pistols has
increased substantially. As a result, the percentage of people who
die after being shot is on the rise. In prior decades, the trend was
moving in the opposite direction as medical care improved. Weapon
caliber has now caught up with medical advances.

These new weapons do not technically violate the National Firearms Act of 1934 and other measures that regulate machine guns,
silencers, short-barreled shotguns, and short-barreled rifles, but
gunmakers are exploiting new technology and finding new loopholes in existing law in order to sell more-lethal weapons, weapons
that Congress intended to stringently regulate and tax. We must

crack down on this behavior by: (1) empowering the government to enforce the existing restrictions; (2) regulating new products designed to get around the laws; (3) prohibiting the sale, purchase, possession, or use of ammunition that poses a particular threat to public safety and has no sport or hunting utility; and (4) ensuring that all products meet safety standards set by the experts at the Consumer Product Safety Commission.

Regulate All Gun Dealers

Believe it or not, gun dealers are not required to keep their guns locked up, so it's no surprise that a gun is stolen in the United States every two minutes. Between 2012 and 2015, according to the FBI, more than 1 million guns were stolen from their owners, and 22,000 were stolen from gun stores. That is nearly half a billion dollars' worth of guns, many of which were used in violent crimes or drug smuggling or entered the arsenal of organized crime.

The Bureau of Alcohol, Tobacco, Firearms and Explosives, usually known as ATF, is the agency that is supposed to regulate and license guns and gun dealers. The bureau is tiny and powerless because for decades the NRA has pressured lawmakers to limit its budget and hamper its operations. As a result, just 14 percent of all gun stores are subject to federal inspection, and none are required to track or report stolen inventory. ATF cannot inspect a gun dealer more than once a year. ATF is not allowed to require gun dealers to conduct an annual inventory to ensure they can account for all of their guns. ATF is so short-staffed that most gun dealers can go five years without ever undergoing inspection. And as a result, once dealers are finally inspected, more than half are found to have some kind of violation. The majority had violations like "missing firearms; failure to verify identification; failure to conduct background checks; failure to stop a sale after purchasers indicated they were prohibited from gun possession; failure to properly keep records of all acquisitions and dispositions."

ATF also lacks the enforcement power it needs to make manufacturers or dealers improve safety. "We can suggest all day long, but ultimately, it comes down to the dealer taking responsibility for their facility and inventory," ATF's deputy assistant director for field operations, Andy Graham, told *The Trace*, a website that reports news on gun-safety efforts.

Gun dealers are frequent targets of "straw purchases" by someone trying to buy a firearm for a prohibited person. Sixty-seven percent said they had experienced at least one straw purchasing attempt in the previous year, and over half agree that current laws make it too easy for criminals to obtain firearms.[1] A majority of the gun industry has adopted security measures to help ensure that guns do not fall into the wrong hands, but ATF does not have the regulatory authority to enforce or monitor safety standards in the industry. Nine states and the District of Columbia have their own laws that push gun dealers to implement better safety practices, but that's clearly not enough.

Stolen guns end up in crime scenes or are diverted into illegal gun trafficking networks and are almost impossible for law enforcement officials to trace, thwarting countless criminal investigations. In large American cities, those markets are important sources of firearms for career criminals. Studies show that significant percentages of those imprisoned for gun crimes were prohibited from legally purchasing guns and turned to unregulated private sellers or found weapons on the black market. Cities with strong gun laws and enforcement often have limited the supply, however. In Chicago, for instance, criminals may pay $400 for a firearm on the black market that costs only $100 from a legal dealer.[2]

Whenever a gun is recovered at a crime scene, staffers at ATF's National Tracing Center face a major challenge. They are prohibited from digitizing sales records in a way that would allow for an easy digital search (the records have to remain in a non-searchable format with the gun dealer). Officials cannot type that gun's serial number into a search engine and pull up records to learn where that gun was purchased and by whom. Instead, staff at the Tracing Center who receive gun serial numbers from law enforcement must call the firearm manufacturer and wholesaler and rely on them to go into their files and dig out that information. Sometimes the tracing center staff must paw through cardboard boxes full of paper records from gun dealers to figure out who owns the gun that law enforcement officials suspect was used in perpetrating the crime. How does this work in the future? Can you imagine a millennial searching a cardboard box to find a piece of actual physical paper?

Besides allowing digital searches, Congress must provide ATF with enough resources to conduct compliance inspections. The Compact would empower ATF to require dealers to implement security measures. It would let the bureau run targeted computer searches on all sales records and fully digitize its operations for the real world.

Reduce the Number of Guns in the United States

America currently has more guns than people. To truly reduce gun violence, restricting the manufacturing and purchase of new firearms is not enough. We must significantly reduce the number of firearms on our streets and in our houses. Doing so will keep people with bad intentions from getting guns already in circulation (likely on the black market) and thus significantly reduce the gun violence. It would also lower suicide rates—as individuals facing personal crisis won't be able to impulsively use a gun to end their lives—and accidental shootings that take place as a result of America's deep immersion in gun culture.

The Compact has a three-pronged approach to achieving this goal: (1) prohibit the sale to civilians of semiautomatic weapons and high-capacity magazines designed for the armed forces; (2) provide incentives for people to give up their existing firearms; and (3) make guns significantly harder to get.

Let's start with the easy part. No one needs assault weapons with ten (or thirty or a hundred) rounds in a single magazine for hunting. No one needs them for target practice. No one needs them to protect their family. No one. These are designed to enable the military to cause death and destruction on a horrific scale.

While a bullet from a regular handgun lacerates an organ, a round from an AR-15-style weapon shreds it, often proving fatal.

The bullets are small, but they leave the muzzle three times faster than a handgun bullet and, as a result, cause far more damage. As one trauma surgeon put it, the damage from an AR-15 "looks like a grenade went off" in the human body; by comparison, the damage from a 9mm handgun "looks like a bad knife cut." If a bullet from an AR-15 hits the liver, "the liver looks like a jello mold that's been dropped on the floor," a trauma surgeon told *Wired*. As it makes its way out of the body, it can leave an exit wound that's the size of an orange.

A quick note on the AR-15: a company called ArmaLite, Inc., developed the weapon in 1956 and it is seen as the civilian version of the U.S. military's M-16 combat rifle. "AR" stands for "ArmaLite Rifle," not "assault rifle" as many people may think. The weapon is a semiautomatic that requires the shooter to pull the trigger for every shot. A large capacity magazine allows an individual to fire many rounds quickly and efficiently without reloading, often leaving destruction in its path.

A review of mass shootings concluded that "incidents where assault weapons or large capacity ammunition magazines were used resulted in 135 percent more people shot and 57 percent more killed, compared to other mass shootings."[1] A more recent study published in *JAMA: The Journal of the American Medical Association* similarly found that in an active-shooter incident, a shooter with a semiautomatic rifle—a larger category of guns than what we typically consider to be "assault weapons"—"may be able to hurt and kill about twice the number of people compared to if they had a non-semiautomatic rifle or a handgun."

In 1994, Congress passed a law that made it unlawful for a person to "manufacture, transfer, or possess" a semiautomatic assault weapon and outlawed the transfer and possession of any new large-capacity ammunition magazines. The measure expired in 2004. During the ten years that it was in effect, manufacturers skirted its

provisions by removing banned features and making small modifica-
tions to existing weapons. They also boosted production of assault
weapons before the ban, thus keeping them in circulation while the
ban was in effect.

Learning from these mistakes, a new assault weapons ban must: (1)
include a one-feature test (meaning that any one of several features
would classify the gun as a prohibited assault weapon); (2) prohibit
the possession, distribution, importation, transportation, manufacture, and sale of assault weapons; and (3) grandfather pre-ban weapons but require their registration and prohibit their sale and transfer.
The most recent proposed federal legislation would ban weapons
that are semiautomatic, capable of accepting detachable magazines,
or have any one design feature, like a folding stock or pistol grip, that
would classify it as an assault weapon. We can also design a better law
by learning from the states. As of 2018, seven states (California, Connecticut, Hawaii, Maryland, Massachusetts, New Jersey, and New
York) and Washington, DC, have banned assault weapons. Each state
offers useful instruction for a federal ban.

Assault weapons have killed a lot of people in mass shootings. But
the truth is, handguns are actually killing far more people. According to a new database by the Department of Homeland Security,
the United States has experienced more than 1,300 school shootings since 1970 and in 68 percent of these shootings the assailant
used a handgun. Assault weapons are also rarely used in low-body-
count homicides and almost never in suicides. In 2016, murderers
used handguns nineteen times more than rifles, and handguns killed
nine times as many people as rifles and shotguns combined. Almost
90 percent of the firearms used to kill 33,000 Americans in 2013 were
handguns.[2] To save lives, we must make handguns far less accessible.
This component of the Compact requires three separate elements.

First, we need a federally funded voluntary gun buyback program
in which an individual can turn in a gun and get money for it—a

version of what the Australians accomplished, which I discuss later. Until now, gun buybacks have shown limited efficacy in the cities and towns where they've been tried. Owners simply turned in guns and used the cash to buy new ones. This is mostly because the supply of firearms is endless and funding for buybacks is limited.

Second, to make this policy work, those who don't voluntarily sell back their guns must be required to obtain a firearms license and register their weapons. People would have to disclose what firearms and ammunition they own, report lost or stolen guns, and undergo realistic inspection and verification. They could sell a firearm only to a licensed individual, and the sale would have to be registered with law enforcement.

The goal here is not to force criminals to do the right thing; they won't. It is to make sure that responsible gun owners, who make up a much higher proportion of the population than professional criminals, are held responsible for their guns. Moreover, firearm registration creates a comprehensive record and lets law enforcement easily trace firearms found at crime scenes to the last legal sale. The policy would also give gun owners an incentive to make sure their guns don't fall into the wrong hands. With registration, it will be traced back to them, after all.

Whenever I bring up the prospect of firearm registration, conservatives push back by claiming that the policy is an unconstitutional abridgment of their Second Amendment rights. "I wouldn't require the press to register their printing presses or obtain a special license to publish," they claim. First of all, words don't kill, at least not directly. Secondly, our rights are not absolute; they come with responsibilities. Even in the context of the First Amendment, those who seek to hold public mass demonstrations must obtain a special license from their city or town and complete documents that are akin to registration. People who seek to change the laws by ballot initiative have to register with the government. Third, the government already compels firearm registration—for certain kinds of guns. Individuals are required to register machine guns and meet other requirements, like fingerprinting, to legally own them. Perhaps that is part of the reason we never hear about machine guns being used in shootings. Yes, the most dedicated of criminals may go to great lengths to commit their crimes, but most are deterred by obstacles that serve as deterrents. That's how all laws work to keep public order and gun regulations are no exception.

The third element of a workable gun-reduction program would be voluntary relinquishment. This could operate outside of a federally funded buyback system and might provide greater flexibility. Instead of sales and paperwork, individuals could simply turn in guns they don't want to a local law enforcement authority. Such a program would be particularly useful for individuals who may inherit large firearm collections from family members or relatives who have passed and are looking for something to do with them.

Believe it or not, no mechanism currently exists for people to turn in their guns. If your gun collector father passes away and you don't want his firearms, the best you could do is sell them. If you're in a crisis situation that's putting you or others at risk, you may just want to get the gun out of there. Today there are few (if any) legally viable options for you to rid yourself of that burden. Voluntary relinquishment would allow people to turn in their guns, no questions asked.

A License to Kill

In the United States, people have to have a license to drive a car or serve liquor in a restaurant. People need a license to cut hair or fish. They should need a license to own a gun.

Gun licensing—along with registration—encourages gun owners to act responsibly and significantly reduces the trafficking of illegal guns. Research has consistently shown that a robust licensing process, which requires a prospective gun owner to visit a local law enforcement authority and complete a background check, keeps us all safer and is essential to building peaceful, gun-free communities.

A study of firearm-related homicides in Connecticut found that the rate "dropped 40 percent after the state adopted a 1995 law that required anyone seeking to buy a handgun to apply for a permit with the local police, complete at least eight hours of safety training, and be 21 years old."[1]

Conversely, after Missouri repealed its licensing law in 2007, gun homicides increased. Individuals no longer had to apply for a permit in person at their local sheriff's office to legally possess a firearm, whether they purchased it from a dealer who had a federal license to sell guns or an individual online.

Immediately after repeal, researchers discovered a substantial increase in gun trafficking and "a sharp increase in the percentage of crime guns recovered by police in Missouri that had been originally sold by in-state retailers."[2] Tragically, the state also saw an increase in the annual firearm homicide rate of 23 percent. Researchers noted that this occurred only for homicides committed with firearms and that a similar spike in firearm deaths did not occur nationally or in states bordering Missouri. Prior to repeal, few guns originating in Missouri had ended up at crime scenes in other states, but after the state did away with the licensing requirement, the number of guns recovered by police in the neighboring states of Iowa and Illinois increased by 37 percent. This trend held even as researchers "controlled for changes in unemployment, poverty, policing levels, incarceration rates, trends in crime reflected in burglary rates, national trends in homicide rates, and several kinds of other laws that could affect homicides."

The newest research on gun licensing, published in the *Journal of Urban Health* in May 2018, showed something more startling: comprehensive background-check laws without a licensing system do *not* appear to decrease firearm homicides. The reasons are fairly obvious. The physical process of obtaining a permit (getting yourself to a law enforcement office, the extended waiting period, the more comprehensive background check) deters bad actors from obtaining firearms.

Without a licensing system, background checks are conducted at the point of sale and are usually less exhaustive, using only a limited number of databases. Even though the overwhelming majority of firearms dealers are responsible, that makes it easier for one to paper over a background check or let a prohibited purchaser buy a firearm. Sellers have a financial incentive to make a sale, and they lack the training to spot fake documents. A government study found that federally licensed gun dealers failed to spot fake IDs from six states, never once questioning their authenticity.[3]

In 2018, ten states required individuals to obtain a license before buying certain firearms and three states required a license to legally own any firearm. Each has different rules, but there are some common denominators. The experiences in these states should serve as a template for designing a federal system.

1. **Prospective gun owners should have to visit a law enforcement office and undergo a background check.** Law enforcement agencies can access a wider array of databases than gun shops to determine if someone is in a prohibited category, and they can take more time to conduct a more robust check. A longer timetable is essential to identify people in crisis and thus reduce the rate of suicide by firearm. Individuals who are convicted of violent crimes, have multiple convictions over a short period of time, or have restraining orders placed against them by a domestic partner should be prohibited from owning a firearm.

2. **Prospective gun owners who apply for a license should be fingerprinted.** This requirement would help reduce sales to people buying for others (prohibited individuals).

3. **Prospective gun owners should be required to complete a robust hands-on training course** in firearms use and safety and pass a written test about the relevant laws. Under the New Second Amendment Compact, the federal government would provide grants to states for training and examinations.

4. **Law enforcement officials should have discretion to deny permits to individuals** who they believe could be dangerous or who attract a great deal of police activity for one reason or another. In fact, states that allow law enforcement discretion in licensing have 76 percent lower per capita rates of firearms exports to criminals in other states; states that do not allow such discretion but do require fingerprints had 45 percent lower

rates.[4] To ensure that this discretion is not abused or differentially applied in a discriminatory manner, individuals should be able to appeal denials through the court system.

5. **Federal gun licenses should be required to be renewed every five years** to ensure that licensees are still eligible to own firearms.

6. **An owner should be required to register the firearm,** report its theft or loss, and store it safely.

Safe storage of guns is essential. When guns are stored without locks or are out in the open, the chance of an accidental, unintentional, or impulsive shooting or a suicide increases dramatically. Unsecured guns are also much more likely to be stolen, sold on the black market, and found at crime scenes.

One 2018 study found that 4.6 million minors live in households with a loaded, unlocked gun. Another concluded that 55 percent of homes that have both firearms and children store their firearms in an unlocked place. Even worse, 43 percent do not have any kind of trigger lock on that firearm.[5]

All of these conditions result in tragedy. Minors who have access to unlocked and unstored firearms are at higher risk for suicide, unintentional injuries, and intentional violence. A government report from 2004 found that, of the school shootings studied, 65 percent were perpetrated by a shooter who got the gun from his home or from a relative's home. (I use the word *his* advisedly here. A table of U.S. mass shootings from 1982 to 2018 shows ninety-eight by males, two by females, and one by a male-female team.[6]) The Department of Education found that "during the 2009–10 school year, one in every 30 K–12 schools took serious disciplinary action against at least one student for use or possession of a firearm on school property."[7]

These numbers are dramatic, but they can be easily reduced. According to one study, states that require that handguns be locked up when not in use experience 68 percent fewer firearm suicides per capita than states that do not. Other researchers estimated that almost one-third of all accidental firearm deaths could be prevented if manufacturers were required to supply and owners were to use a childproof safety lock or a loading indicator that shows when the weapon is loaded with live ammunition.

Massachusetts is the only state that generally requires firearms to be stored with a lock in place, and it has significantly lower rates of gun deaths than other states as a result. Nationally, 39 percent of youths who commit suicide use guns; in Massachusetts, that number is just 9 percent.

California, Connecticut, and New York all impose safe-storage requirements in certain situations, and all have "40 percent fewer suicides per capita and 68 percent fewer firearm suicides per capita than states without these laws. This correlation is unchanged even after controlling for the effects of poverty, population density, age, education, and race/ethnicity."[8] With numbers like these, is there any reason we would not require any federal licensing law to follow the model set out by these four?

Individuals with federal licenses to own firearms should be able to upgrade their licenses to carry their firearms outside the home. Carrying concealed firearms in public creates a heightened level of risk and should require additional responsibilities. In urban areas, concealed carry is associated with a 14 percent increase in firearm homicides, so gun owners who wish to carry weapons outside the home should have to pass additional field and safety tests to receive this special certification.[9] If they do, they should be able to carry concealed firearms anywhere in the country.

Currently, states have different rules and standards for concealed-carry permits. Some require background checks and training; others do not require anything at all.

The NRA is working to make things even worse. It is advancing "concealed carry reciprocity," which would require all states to recognize the concealed-carry permits of every other state. Under this scheme, a state like New York, which has very stringent requirements for receiving a permit—you must be of good moral character and demonstrate proper cause but can still be denied a permit by the issuing officer—would have to honor permits from a state like Idaho. In Idaho, almost any person who is at least eighteen years old can carry a concealed weapon, no questions asked. Since studies have found that weak permitting rules increase violent crime by 13 to 15 percent, residents in states with tougher rules worry that inviting armed out-of-staters would put them in harm's way. Police departments and police associations also oppose this NRA proposal, arguing that it endangers their lives and would make it difficult for a police officer to identify individuals carrying unlawfully.

We must prevent a race to the bottom and set a solid federal floor, for both the ownership license and the concealed-carry supplement. Individuals with these federal documents would be able to own and/or carry their weapon anywhere in the United States. However, states that wish to adopt even tougher standards to meet their unique needs should be free to do so. If a state like Massachusetts adopts tougher standards than the national floor, it would still recognize out-of-state licenses that meet the federal rules. Massachusetts residents, however, would have to fulfill the additional state requirements to receive a license in the state.

Gun licensing is so common sense that 70 percent of Americans believe that a gun licensing system already exists. This is an easy one.

Insure Your Piece

If you are going to own a firearm, you should insure it. You buy insurance for your car to protect yourself and other drivers from liability. You buy home owner's insurance when you take out a mortgage. You buy renter's insurance when you rent a property. You cannot practice as a lawyer or a doctor without liability insurance. Owning a gun is just as important a responsibility.

Insurance provides us all with financial security in case of an accident that damages you or others. It guarantees that you will not go bankrupt paying for those damages and ensures that your victim has a means of compensation as well. Insurance also discourages people from acting recklessly. A thoughtless act or even a no-fault accident may cause the insurer to charge you higher premiums; it may revoke coverage altogether for high-risk individuals with long-standing patterns of troubling behavior. On the other hand, years of claim-free living could lower your premiums over time.

Insurance companies also collect data about people's behavior and the claims they file, information that can reveal important patterns and insights for saving lives. Insurers have an incentive to mitigate risk, and they conduct research about how individuals can act more responsibly, sometimes even launching public campaigns encouraging people to do so or lobbying Congress to adopt sensible policies.

Requiring liability insurance for firearm ownership would create a series of positive incentives that would help achieve the goal of a future with fewer guns.

Store your guns safely, enroll in a gun-safety course, purchase a less dangerous firearm, go without any incidents for a long period of time, and you will benefit from insurance discounts; use guns in a way that leads to gun accidents, and you will pay a higher price. It's about time people had some financial skin in the game and victims of gun crimes or accidents had a clear path to compensation.

The Compact proposes that states require liability insurers to offer insurance for gun owners and that those who choose to own a firearm be insured. States could also consider mandating that a portion of insurance premiums be diverted into a special compensation fund for victims.[1]

Insurance could help reduce the two-thirds of gun deaths that are suicides by increasing the delay between purchase and firearm acquisition, imposing a waiting period that would have some impact on the suicide rate, as people in crisis are far less likely to kill themselves once the moment of crisis has passed. Insurers may also develop screening mechanisms for denying liability insurance to high-risk individuals, thus depriving them of an efficient way to kill themselves. All of that is good news.

While the benefits of insurance are clear, some natural obstacles arise. Insurance policies may cover only a fraction of gun deaths, most obviously accidental discharges. Those make up approximately 2 percent of all gun deaths.

The question is: can an insurance company insure a gun owner who uses a firearm to commit intentional harm—the 35 percent or so of gun deaths that result from assault or homicide? In other words, if someone shoots me, would the insurance company have to pay out a claim that covers my medical bills? Would insurers have to cover that kind of criminal behavior?

Short answer: it's possible. Insurers do already insure against illegal acts. Automobile insurance policies, for instance, provide coverage for bodily injury or property damage when people drive under the influence of drugs or alcohol. These are criminal acts that insurance companies cover because there are so many of them and they occur so frequently. Excluding coverage for driving while under the influence, therefore, would defeat the purpose of insurance and deny compensation to victims.

Now, to be sure, an insurance policy cannot prevent someone from premeditating a shooting. If other psychological factors and deterrents are not stopping you from killing someone, an insurance policy certainly will not. However, gun-crime insurance could provide a revenue stream for dealing with the economic consequences of gun violence. Some estimates place that price tag at over $100 billion per year for lost wages, medical bills, depressed property values, and increased costs to the criminal justice system.[2] If insurance policies can help defray some of those societal costs—by forcing us to take some degree of personal responsibility for our actions—would we not all be better off?

End Armed Intimidation

Gun advocates carry guns in public spaces to protest gun restrictions, assert their Second Amendment rights, and intimidate and confuse people. When my boyfriend traveled to Houston, Texas, on a business trip in the summer of 2018, he was shocked to learn that individuals could openly carry their firearms in public and feverishly texted me to ask if they could do so legally.

In 2018, partly as a result of NRA lobbying, in thirty-one states people could carry firearms without any license or permit; fifteen states required some form of license. Forty-four states allow openly carrying rifles and shotguns, though some do have restrictions.

In urban areas, there is almost no reason to openly brandish a firearm. Open carry frightens citizens going to the store, to church, or to their favorite restaurant, and, most important, it intimidates those who are hoping to exercise their constitutional right to vote. Moreover, both concealed and open carry tend to escalate misunderstandings into manslaughter.

Open carry has a long and complicated racial history, one that once pushed gun enthusiasts to embrace the very kind of restrictions they so vehemently oppose today.

On May 2, 1967, thirty members of the Black Panther Party legally entered the California statehouse carrying firearms. They did so to protest the Mulford Act, a measure drafted to allow only law enforcement officials to walk around with loaded guns in public. The legislature was debating the measure after the Panthers began patrolling the streets of Oakland, California, to combat the injustices they were facing at the hands of white people.

At the capitol that day, the armed group was disarmed and escorted out in thirty minutes. Nobody was hurt, but newspapers throughout the country seized on the event, calling it the Sacramento Invasion. Predictably, white citizens began to call for restrictions on open carry.

The California legislature fast-tracked the Mulford Act. The bill cleared a key committee after its sponsor testified that it had the support of the NRA, and passed with bipartisan support. Days later, it was signed into law by Governor Ronald Reagan.

Over fifty years later, little has changed. White America is still freaked out by black people with firearms. As a result, African American men pay the ultimate price for carrying guns (or objects that resemble guns), a threat that middle-aged suburban white men, the majority of open carriers, rarely confront. In open-carry Ohio, for instance, Tamir Rice, a twelve-year-old African American, was killed for holding a pellet gun. John Crawford III, an African American man, was shot dead by police for holding an air rifle he picked off the shelf at Walmart. A police officer shot and killed Philando Castile during a routine traffic stop, even after Castile informed him he was legally carrying a gun.

As we shift toward a culture with fewer guns, states must prohibit open carry. The fewer guns in public, the safer the public is.

Unleash the Power of Science
to Save Lives

The United States spends $240 million a year on traffic safety research. That research—which helped improve car and road safety—has saved 360,000 lives since 1970 and produced a 28 percent reduction in the rate of annual car accident deaths between 1999 and 2014.

We rely on science to solve the ever-evolving challenges presented by driver behavior on our roads. For instance, in 2012, federally funded researchers learned that texting and other driver distractions played a role in over three thousand car deaths. In response, almost all of the fifty states banned driving while texting. Two years later, a study found that such laws resulted in a lower rate of deaths among young drivers.[1]

Imagine how many lives we could save if our government funded scientific research into the best ways to reduce gun violence. Right now, in most cases, it does not.

In 1996 the NRA pressured Congress to pass a legislative rider that virtually banned federal dollars from funding scientific research about gun violence as part of that year's spending bill, and Congress has renewed the rider ever since.[2] Why? It's obvious. The research would almost certainly corroborate and extend previous research showing that many guns are too dangerous for the civilian market, increasing pressure to shrink the marketplace for gun manufacturers and require the industry to adopt new safety measures.

Screw industry profits! Life is more important. We must invest heavily in research and develop an ambitious agenda to unlock the potential of science to save thousands of lives. Here are key questions that deserve scientific answers:

- How do guns make their way onto crime scenes?
- What are the risk factors for gun violence and what are the best ways to address them? In particular, why are nearly all shootings committed by men, and what does this gender gap tell us about solutions?
- How do individuals who commit gun crimes obtain their guns?
- What is the best way to design guns to make them safer?
- How can community leaders intervene in high-crime communities and prevent gun violence before it takes innocent lives?
- What is the best way to intervene in personal crises to prevent suicides?
- What is the best way to prevent and respond to mass shootings?

The federal government should invest at least $10 million in gun safety research. This should be as obvious as pumping far greater sums into a cure for cancer or Alzheimer's disease.

Even the original author of the research restriction, the late representative Jay Dickey, had a change of heart about the ban and had urged Congress to allow federal funding for gun studies. "Research could have been continued on gun violence without infringing on the rights of gun owners, in the same fashion that the highway industry continued its research without eliminating the automobile . . . it is my position that somehow or some way we should slowly but methodically fund such research until a solution is reached," he told reporters in 2017. "Doing nothing is no longer an acceptable solution."[3]

Reducing Gun Violence in Chicago

In 2000, an epidemiologist named Gary Slutkin, who spent his career fighting epidemics in Africa, began to apply the science-based strategies of disease control to urban violence. Slutkin recognized that homicides in U.S. cities occurred in clusters in particular neighborhoods, just like infectious disease outbreaks. The violence came and went in particular seasons and occurred in response to other violence, just as the flu or other diseases that are spread from one person to another.

"We see violence, in a way, behaving like a contagious process," Gary explained in a TED (Technology, Entertainment, and Design) Talk in 2013, occurring because of fights, gang wars, or mere disagreements. The key, he found, was to adapt the well-established process that doctors and global health experts use for reversing a health epidemic—interrupting transmission, preventing future spread, and changing group norms.

The program works like this: Say a macho guy is insulted at a party. He may plan to retaliate with a gun. His friends and associates react to slights with violence, and he has learned this behavior from them. A violent reply is simply an expected and familiar norm.

This is where Slutkin's violence interrupters come in. They are themselves community members; they may be friends with the angry man or people he spends time with. The trained interrupters hang around the neighborhood. They hear about the planned retaliation and approach the hothead. Initially, he may show little interest in discussing the problem, but the trained interrupters persist. They work to cool him down, keep him occupied, and validate his complaints. They are there to buy time, to shift his perspective, and help him to feel good about himself outside of a violent context. The interrupters may spend weeks or months with the guy, working to shift his perspective so he doesn't relapse into violence the next time a disagreement arises. The program's ultimate goal is to shift the norms of the community as those whose violence is interrupted begin to set a new standard of behavior for their peers. Next time Macho Man hears a friend threaten to kill someone, he himself may interfere and work to calm his friend down, thus helping to slowly shift the expected community reply from assault to more peaceful conflict resolution strategies.

Slutkin first applied his technique to West Garfield, Chicago, one of the most violent neighborhoods in Chicago at the turn of the century. This first experiment resulted in a 67 percent drop in homicides, and the program has achieved similar results throughout the country. The initiative, known as Cure Violence, is now active in more than fifty cities all around the world, where it has led to 41 to 73 percent drops in shootings and killings, transforming whole neighborhoods. Slutkin and his team have since worked to stop cartel violence in South America and tribe and militia violence in Iraq, and they are piloting an initiative to reduce violent recruitment in North Africa.

Efforts to build peaceful environments with fewer guns operate on the principle that the entire community, not just law enforcement, must play a role in stopping gun crime. They are rooted in reality. Because guns are ubiquitous and are not going away any time soon, we must change individual and community standards of behavior.

Some violence intervention programs feature meetings between, on the one hand, groups of people most likely to perpetrate gun violence and, on the other, religious and business leaders, police officers, and community elders. At these meetings, the peaceable people urge the actual and potential shooters to end the attacks. They're told that if they don't, the entire community will cooperate with law enforcement to address the problem and impose swift and certain consequences on the entire group. Research has found that individuals are more likely to recognize authority when they see it as acting on behalf of (or even at the request of) the community, rather than as an external force void of community buy-in and participation.

Other successful intervention programs are aimed at teaching young people how to make better decisions and avoid ever picking up the gun in the first place. In Chicago, the Becoming a Man (BAM) program trains ninth- and tenth-grade boys to pause and think before they act. "Sometimes people make decisions based on automatic thinking in situations where that automatic response is not appropriate, particularly if you live in an environment where the situations are changing quickly and where the consequences for making the wrong decision are very large," says economist Jonathan Guryan, who assessed the program's effectiveness.

BAM starts with an exercise in which participants are divided into pairs. One holds a ball in his hand, and the other has one minute to take it from him. Most young men try to wrestle the ball out of the other's hand or otherwise use physical force to get it. The program leader then asks them all a simple question. Did anybody just *ask* for the ball? Few, if any, students raise their hands. Usually, each claims his partner wouldn't have given up the ball or would have viewed him as weak if he had merely asked for it. The student originally holding the ball usually disagrees, saying he would have handed it over. This simple exercise teaches students the danger of making assumptions about others and the value of pausing to assess a situation before acting. Guryan and his colleagues have found that students who participate in the initiative are 50 percent less likely to be involved in violent crime than those who don't and have better grades and graduation rates.

Programs like these can work in tandem with those that connect gun violence victims in hospitals with social workers and case managers who provide them with social services in their hour of need and help them overcome the desire for revenge after they recover. These models have already reduced homicide rates by 30 to 60 percent and would likely show even more success if they became a government priority and received a steady stream of federal funding. The funds could be administered by state or city governments and invested in health departments and community-based organizations that specialize in coordinating such initiatives. Slutkin estimates that 50 to 80 percent of the gun violence problem would be resolved by an investment of a few billion dollars, a drop in the bucket when compared to the hundreds of billions our nation loses each year to incarceration, policing, lawyers and court costs, economic disruption, medical treatment of traumatic wounds, and the downstream problems of families torn asunder by gun violence.

As part of these efforts, the government, working with the community, nonprofits, and private entities, must invest in at-risk individuals by providing social, educational, and economic assistance. Most urban gun violence is perpetrated by small groups from the poorest, most underserved communities. There, guns are essential for protection in an underground economy. These people need help—transportation support, tutoring, and access to health care, housing, and GED classes. Thriving schools and strong families are some of the most important tools for fighting and reducing crime. Directly investing in underserved communities on the federal, state, and local levels is absolutely essential to address the root causes of urban gun violence. Conservatives who object to spending tax dollars on the poor fail to understand that the potential social and economic benefits for all of us far outweigh the expenditures.

All of these programs would be even more effective if implemented alongside the other policies included in the Compact. We should be investing in underserved communities while instituting reforms that tightly regulate firearm dealers and impose a federal licensing and registration system to prevent guns from flowing into their neighborhoods. About 60 percent of crime guns recovered in Chicago come from states like Indiana, where gun regulations are incredibly lax and firearms are easy to come by.[1] In 2014, over 90 percent of crime guns recovered in New York came from out of state, and half came from the ten states with the weakest gun laws.[2] Tough federal standards would end this deadly traffic.

How to Eliminate Mass Shootings

It was a sunny morning in April when a tall, slender, long-haired twenty-eight-year-old man named Martin Bryant hopped into a yellow Volvo 240 GL station wagon with a surfboard on its roof. He carried a sports bag filled with clothes, a towel, handcuffs, rope, a hunting knife, three semiautomatic weapons, and a significant quantity of ammunition. Martin was not out to catch some waves. Instead, he drove to a charming white cottage that was used as a guesthouse, walked in, gagged, stabbed, and fatally shot its two elderly keepers. The couple were family acquaintances whom Martin faulted for contributing to his father's suicide by outbidding the Bryants for the property where both now lay dead. Martin had exacted his revenge.

He quickly locked the doors to the guesthouse and sped off to a café that catered to tourists. It was about to become the scene of one of the most gruesome mass killings in modern history.

Before killing more, however, Martin had a light lunch with some fruit juice outside on the Broad Arrow Café balcony. The killer wore his blond wavy hair shoulder length. He was described as awkwardly nervous, constantly glancing back at his yellow Volvo from the balcony. Speaking aloud to no one in particular, he tried to get other diners to join him in decrying the lack of WASPs (white Anglo Saxon Protestants) in the area and the low number of Japanese tourists that season.

Feeling full, he stood up, walked from the balcony back into the café, and placed his sports bag on an empty table. Out of it came a Colt AR-15 rifle, which Martin had purchased through a private newspaper ad. He fitted it with a thirty-shot magazine and approximately twenty-six rounds of ammunition. He would later describe the weapon to authorities as "a sweet little gun."

Shots rang out suddenly, giving people little time to react, much less flee. The first two bullets killed a couple visiting from Malaysia. The third struck a young man in the top of the head. The fourth killed his girlfriend. The bullets just kept on coming, loud bangs in rapid succession.

Some tourists initially believed the noise to be part of a historical reenactment and moved toward the sound, only to recoil at the carnage before them: people being knocked down like bowling pins by a gun that seemed to emit an endless stream of bullets. Several patrons tried to distract the killer with sudden movements and loud noises, driven by sheer human instinct to protect each other. Others hid under tables and in dark corners, paralyzed by a "fatalistic acceptance that they were likely to be the next to be shot." A mother covered her daughter with her body. She was shot in the back and suffered a ruptured eardrum from the noise of the shot, but she survived. The daughter she had selflessly sought to protect did not.

A sense of helplessness came over the crowd as Martin continued to walk from one table to the other, shooting his "sweet little gun" at close range and "laughing in an aggressive way," witnesses later recalled. In two minutes, he fired twenty-nine shots, killing twenty people and injuring twelve.

Suddenly bored, Martin turned his focus outside, where café staffers and patrons had escaped and were now alerting pedestrians to the horror unfolding inside. Some hid behind one of the four tourist buses parked on the street. The shuttles proved no safer than the café.

Martin popped down to his car, dumped the AR-15, and picked up his Canadian Army version of the Belgian Fabrique Nationale SLR (self-loading rifle). He began to fire indiscriminately at the tourists, walking around one coach, then the next. To the dismay of those seeking refuge, Martin hopped inside the buses, killing four people huddled in the seats and injuring six more. His death toll was now at twenty-four.

He got back into his Volvo, started the engine, and drove away from the scene, beeping his horn and waving.

Nanette Mikac, a young mother, and her two children, Madeline (three years old) and Alannah (six), were walking quickly on foot away from the carnage. Nanette had Madeline in her arms, while Alannah was running alongside, her short legs working to keep up with her mother's determined pace. "We're safe now, Pumpkin," Nanette told her older daughter. The words eased Alannah's anxiety, and she moved closer to her mother, looking up at her.

At that moment, the yellow Volvo appeared from down the road. Martin slowed down and opened the door. Nanette approached him, believing him to be a stranger offering a ride. To her horror, Martin stepped out of the car with his AR-15, put his hand on her shoulder, and ordered her to her knees. "Please don't hurt my babies," she pleaded. Without flinching, Martin released a round into her temple. She died immediately. He turned around and pointed his gun at Madeline, shooting her twice and killing her, too. Alannah, meanwhile, was trying to get away and had run behind a tree. Martin chased her down, pressed the AR-15's muzzle against the right side of her neck, and executed her.

Martin had now murdered twenty-seven people at the café and in the surrounding area.

He made his way back to the white cottage, terrorizing anyone he encountered. He murdered four people in a BMW and carjacked their vehicle. He killed a woman exiting a gas station and locked a man inside his car trunk. Back at the cottage, he poured gasoline over the BMW, pulling his hostage out before setting it ablaze.

For the next eighteen hours, Martin locked himself inside the cottage and, in a series of incoherent calls with police—Martin identified himself as "Jamie"—requested a helicopter. Eventually, his phone lost charge and he stopped communicating. At some point, he set fire to the cottage and ran out of it "naked and staggering for a little way before dropping to his knees." He had surrendered himself to police.

The bodies of the hostage and the two innkeepers were "burnt beyond recognition; identification was confirmed by means of dental records and DNA analysis," the police said. All that was left was the AR-15.

In the weeks that followed, the two guns played a central role in the public debate surrounding the tragedy. As newspapers and TV stations throughout the country memorialized the victims in around-the-clock coverage, the public began to ask how a civilian could legally purchase weapons powerful enough to kill thirty-five and injure twenty-three so rapidly. Just hours after news of the shooting broke on television and radio, the nation's most prominent gun-safety organizations issued statements calling on the government "to take immediate action and show leadership" by enacting stricter gun regulations, urging leaders to seize the moment and pass a package of reforms that, they argued, would help prevent such a tragedy from ever occurring again. They had been pressing this case for years, only to be rebuffed time and again by the nation's powerful gun lobby, which had a near stranglehold on lawmakers.

In the days following the massacre, gun lobby spokespeople expressed their thoughts and prayers for the victims and their families but insisted that neither gun owners nor the availability of guns could be blamed for the horrific event. They urged the authorities to focus on why Martin, who appeared to have had developmental challenges, had not been identified by law enforcement officials as a potential threat. They maintained that the actions of one madman should not limit regular people's access to firearms, for doing so was "an invasion of law-abiding citizens' rights," besides being "undemocratic" and a threat to citizens' right to self-defense. Gun control reforms were "attacking the wrong end of the problem while ignoring the real causes of violence," alleged to be media glorification of criminals and a broken system that failed to screen out mentally unstable people from gun ownership.

The lobby warned of gun confiscations and flooded lawmakers with letters and phone calls threatening to vote them out of office if they dared to support stricter gun laws. Some legislators even received death threats. The gun lobby acted just like the NRA.

Gun reform advocates and the gun lobby had dug into familiar territory, reading off scripts like actors who had memorized and mastered their lines. Then suddenly—to everyone's surprise—the performance went awry, the play was upended, and the country's trajectory was forever changed. Led by the Conservative government of Prime Minister John Howard, Australia responded to the mass shooting by adopting some of the most restrictive gun laws the world had ever seen.

The massacre in the previous pages took place at Port Arthur, Australia, a former convict settlement and one of the country's most beloved heritage sites. The significance of the site and the enormity of the tragedy woke up a nation that until 1996 was home to a gun culture rivaled only by that of the United States.

For decades, Australia had been moving culturally and socially away from the traditions of Great Britain and toward the societal and political norms of the United States. Both countries were home to a robust gun culture, fed by a frontier spirit skeptical of government interventions and restrictions. Both countries had powerful gun lobbies (at the time, Australia's lobby consisted of three main groups, which were funded, at least in part, by the NRA) that aggressively preserved and presented the image of gun owners as "salt of the earth farmers who owned guns for recreation or self defense." Both countries had lawmakers wary of upsetting this powerful rural constituency; they saw gun crimes as an inevitable by-product of modern society, unstoppable because there would always be bad guys with guns.

In spite of these parallels, just twelve days after the Port Arthur massacre, Australia's Conservative prime minister—one of the most conservative politicians in the country's history—decided to solve a problem that had been plaguing his country for years: too many firearms in private hands. He pulled together a broad coalition of supporters to promote the most comprehensive set of gun reforms in modern history. The measure was adopted in all of the country's eight states and territories.

Under Australia's National Firearms Agreement (NFA), all firearms had to be registered as part of an integrated shooter licensing scheme. Semiautomatic weapons like the ones used by Martin to kill thirty-five people were banned. Those who sought to buy a weapon had to provide a "genuine reason" for owning a firearm and apply for a license. Most important, the government *required* individuals to surrender the guns now declared illegal and offered full market value for them. Under the terms of the buyback, Australians had to sell their weapons to the government during a twelve-month period at the average of prices listed in gun dealers' catalogs or face a serious criminal penalty. Most people complied, turning in more than 640,000 weapons during the first buyback and eventually giving up a million. The first buyback eliminated an estimated one-third of the nation's private arsenal.

In the eighteen years before Australia implemented its reforms, the nation experienced thirteen mass shootings; since then, it has not had any large public mass killings. With fewer guns in circulation, the national rate of gun homicide plunged to 0.13 per 100,000. Before Port Arthur, the national rate of gun homicide was one-fifteenth of the U.S. rate; it is now twenty-seven times lower than that of the United States.

The most comprehensive study of Australia's reforms found that "the buyback led to a drop in the firearm suicide rates of almost 80 percent, with no significant effect on non-firearm death rates." The probability that one would die from a gunshot plummeted by 50 percent, and the annual gun homicide total fell by 130 percent. Further research concluded that buying back 3,500 guns per 100,000 people "correlated with up to a 50 percent drop in firearm homicides and a 74 percent drop in gun suicides."[1]

After decades of inaction, Australia responded to a national tragedy by building a future with fewer guns. It chose to act. Even though Australia's pre-reform gun-death rate was much lower than America's and its population is much smaller, that choice saved hundreds, perhaps thousands, of lives.

The NRA has spread and continues to spread lies about the Australian experience. It produced a video claiming that crime rates skyrocketed after reform. In response, Australia's attorney general wrote a letter to the NRA president, saying, "There are many things that Australia can learn from the United States. How to manage firearm ownership is not one of them. . . . I request you withdraw immediately the misleading information from your latest campaign." Needless to say, that video is still being circulated online.

How can the United States make that same choice? Why have we not acted to prevent mass shootings? What lessons can our Aussie neighbors offer to a country still awash with guns and gun violence?

To find out the answer, I called up Philip Alpers, a longtime Australian gun researcher who has also worked on gun safety in the

United States. What, I wondered, had been the tipping point in Australia?

"Voter revolt. Voter disgust. Voter pressure. That is what changed it. Port Arthur was merely the last straw. We already had, over thirteen or fifteen years, ten to fifteen mass shootings" (in a population about one-fourteenth that of America's) during which the country had conducted over a dozen very high-profile parliamentary inquiries, he told me. Every commission issued the same set of recommendations. Every commission's recommendations "were ignored, ignored, ignored, largely because of the pressure of the gun lobby."

It took a mass shooting of the size of Port Arthur for the public mood to change, to turn against the gun lobby and, to some degree, gun owners themselves. That cultural shift, Alpers explained, was the biggest change in Australian society and laid the groundwork for the legal reforms. Before the massacre, gun owners were seen as "salt of the earth, good blokes." After, Australians realized that "gun owners were perfectly legal blokes right up until the moment they were not."

"Ordinary Australians realized that gun owners are just like the rest of us, could get just as mentally unstable, just as drunk, just as angry, as any other Australian male," Alpers added. The problem was, they had deadly weapons.

That realization may have swayed Prime Minister Howard to boldly declare his intention to pursue uniform gun laws, despite initial skepticism from members of his own government. Howard cast his embrace of reform in starkly personal terms, but his decision to buck his natural constituency, the gun lobby and rural Australian voters, provided bipartisan cover for liberal parties and allowed them to support reform without fear that it could be used against them in the next election. As one Australian parliamentarian explained, "We go into public life to try to make things better, but then politics gets in the way. It is good to get the chance to do what is right without worrying about politics."

Lawmakers' fears were also eased by the hundreds of community organizations that came together in support of tighter gun laws, catapulting the issue from the purview of a single political lobby into the mainstream of Australian politics. "Public health and medical societies, women's groups, senior citizens' associations, rural counselors, youth agencies, parents' groups, legal services, human rights organizations, churches, researchers, trade unions, and police" all argued that, while guns can be used for legitimate purposes like hunting and sport, they are *designed* to be dangerous and so are a threat to public health and safety.

Australia also had one other motivating factor that we Americans do not: Americans. "As much as Australians admire and love things that go on in the U.S., they do not identify or support America's infatuation and infestation of firearms," Alpers said. In 1996, as the country was embroiled in debating the proposed reform package offered by the Howard government, "if you stopped people on the street and did vox pops [Australian slang for man-on-the-street interviews] on gun laws, they would say, 'We do not want to go the American way, we do not want to be like America.'" In fact, in the hours after the Port Arthur shooting, Australia's gun-safety coalition issued a press release calling on the government to adopt stricter gun reforms and avoid following America's example:

> The Coalition for Gun Control has called on the Prime Minister to take immediate action and show leadership to prevent Australia going further down the American road of increasing levels of gun violence. Mr. Howard must act tomorrow to announce national uniform gun registration; a ban on private ownership of semi-automatics; steep annual licence and registration fees; and far tougher guidelines on who can own firearms.

The American road! Australians identified high rates of gun violence as uniquely American. News reports of America's high homicide rate gave Australians what one author described as "a strong sense of America going down a violent road of no return." Howard himself, a close friend of the Bush family, echoed this line as he traveled the country to promote his plan. This package of reforms "means that this country through its governments has decided not to go down the American path, but this country has decided to go down another path," Howard said in his address to the nation.

Decades after enacting some of the world's toughest gun laws and building a country with fewer guns, Australia has enjoyed a reduction in homicides and suicides while still maintaining a vibrant gun culture. Hundreds of thousands of Australians own guns and continue to use them safely every day on their farms and in their orchards for perfectly legitimate reasons. Australia demonstrates that instituting gun controls does not mean the death of the gun culture.

Many Americans like to think of the United States as exceptional, with nothing to learn from anyone else, but there is no shame in America now looking to its global neighbors to embrace the reforms that have gotten guns off the streets and out of houses, saving many lives. Australia constructed a future with fewer guns and, as I outline in the pages ahead, we *must* learn from its example if we too wish to live without mass gun violence.

The Solutions in the Compact Have Worked in the Rest of the World

In 2016, Adam Lankford, a political scientist at the University of Alabama, had a simple question: why does the United States have more public mass shootings in its schools, workplaces, churches, mosques, theaters, and public restaurants than other developed countries around the world? To find the answer, Lankford sorted through publicly available data from 171 countries, studying all variables that could possibly explain this phenomenon.

He gathered data on firearm ownership rates, GDP per capita, levels of urbanization, population density, ratio of men to women, and many other factors, then ran a statistical analysis. The stats clearly showed that countries with higher firearm ownership rates have more public mass shooters. The United States is far and away number one in firearm ownership rate and total number of civilian-owned firearms—and massacres. In fact, we are such an outlier among developed nations that Lankford ran an analysis that excluded the United States and just studied the patterns in the other 170 countries. Would the relationship hold? he wondered. The answer was yes. Even when you take the United States out of the equation, firearm ownership is still directly related to the number of mass shootings.

Nineteen years earlier, researchers at the University of

California–Berkeley, working with a slightly different data set—violence as opposed to just mass shootings—had concluded something similar. They found that the United States does not have higher crime rates than our global peers; our crime is just far more lethal, resulting in more deaths. "A series of specific comparisons of the death rates from property crime and assault in New York City and London show how enormous differences in death risk can be explained even while general patterns are similar," the researchers wrote.[1] "A preference for crimes of personal force and the willingness and ability to use guns in robbery make similar levels of property crime fifty-four times as deadly in New York City as in London."

Between 2010 and 2014, Philadelphia had an annual homicide rate of 18.8 per 100,000; Chicago, 16.3; and New York, 5.1. London, by comparison, had a rate of just 1.4 per 100,000 over the same period.[2]

"I really think the issue is with how easy is it for someone to get a firearm in a given country. So firearm ownership rates are kind of approximating that or estimating it," Lankford said. Over the last several decades, gun ownership rates may have declined, but access to guns has increased, and more and more firearms are concentrated in the hands of fewer people. It is now easier than ever to obtain a gun in the United States, and a high percentage of mass shooters actually obtain their weapons legally.

A 2017 survey of gun ownership found that the United States has an estimated 393,300,000 guns in civilian circulation, or 120.5 guns per 100 residents.[3] The country with the next largest number of civilian guns is India at a little over 71 million (0.054 guns per 100), followed by China at close to 50 million civilian firearms (0.036 guns per 100). We have about 3,347 times as many guns per capita as China. Americans make up approximately 5 percent of the world population, but we have some 46 percent of the world's civilian-owned firearms and, not coincidentally, from 1966 to 2012, we were also home to 31 percent of all mass shootings. In 2016, the United States was one of six countries that, collectively, contributed to more than half of all gun deaths worldwide. Together, the United States, Brazil, Mexico, Colombia, Venezuela, and Guatemala represent less than 10 percent of the global population but endure more than half of the entire world's gun deaths.

Americans are twenty-five times more likely to be murdered by a gun than our peers in twenty-two other high-income countries, eight times more likely to commit suicide, and six times more likely to die of an unintentional shooting.[4] Traveling outside of those twenty-two nations to the rest of the world does not paint a prettier picture.

- The United States has a higher rate of gun deaths than any of the twenty-three countries in western Europe.
- The United States has a higher rate of gun deaths than all but one of the twenty-one countries in eastern Europe.
- The United States has a higher rate of gun deaths than all but one of the countries in the Middle East.
- The United States has a higher rate of gun deaths than all but two of the nineteen countries in Southeast Asia, East Asia, and Australia.
- Only seven of forty-three countries in sub-Saharan Africa have higher rates of gun death than the United States.

Almost every other developed country has responded to these truths by restricting access to firearms (usually following an instance of mass shooting) and by adopting the kind of reforms that Australia championed and that I lay out in the Compact: licensing, registration, background checks, firearm restrictions, and safety requirements, just to name a few.

GLOBAL MORTALITY FROM FIREARMS IN SELECTED COUNTRIES

	United States	Canada	Australia	Israel	United Kingdom	Japan	Germany
Deaths per 100,000	10.6	2.1	1.0	2.1	0.3	0.2	0.9
Civilian firearms per 100	120.5	34.7	14.7	6.7	4.6*	0.3	19.6
Licensing		*	*		*	*	*
Background check		*	*	*	*	*	*
Safety course		*		*		*	*
Guns restricted		*	*	*	*	*	
Buyback program			*		*		*
Registry		*	*	*		*	*
Must show need			*	*	*		*
Storage rules		*	*	*	*	*	*

*Number only for England and Wales.

Gun Reforms Around the World

United Kingdom: Following a school shooting in 1996—during which a legally armed gunman killed a teacher and sixteen five- and six-year-old children and injured thirteen more—Parliament banned all handguns within two years. The change came in the midst of increasing crime rates and a growing perception that "American-style" gun culture was taking hold in Britain. As a result, the National Ballistics Intelligence Service reports fewer guns on the streets. In 2012, Great Britain experienced just thirty-two gun homicides.

Brazil: Brazil has the highest number of annual gun deaths. In 2003, the country responded to growing urban violence with a comprehensive measure that banned civilians from carrying weapons, banned certain weapons, raised the legal age for gun ownership, and established a database of gun owners. That and multiple voluntary government-sponsored gun buyback programs have reduced gun deaths and saved more than five thousand lives. According to Brazil's Ministry of Health, the effort has taken half a million guns off the streets, and gun deaths have fallen by 70 percent in São Paulo and 30 percent in Rio de Janeiro.

Canada: In December 1989, a student armed with a semi-automatic rifle killed fourteen students and injured twelve others at a Montreal engineering school. In response, Canada passed the 1995 Firearms Act, which requires licensing, registration, and names of three personal references. In addition, applicants have to take a safety course and pass a comprehensive background check during a mandatory sixty-day waiting period. Restricted weapons, like assault rifles, are allowed only if one completes an additional safety course and demonstrates need, as for target shooting competitions.

Germany: Following two school shootings in 2003 and 2009, Germany passed severe restrictions on gun ownership. Germany is now the only country in the world where people under the age of twenty-five are required to pass a psychiatric exam before even applying for a gun license and licensees are subject to a yearlong waiting period. Police are permitted to conduct unannounced spot checks to ensure that guns are properly locked and stored. These policies have contributed to a 25 percent reduction in gun crimes from 2010 to 2015.[5]

Most of the developed world has embraced a public health approach to gun violence, which seeks to limit gun deaths by changing not the behavior of individual shooters, but the environment in which they operate. Rather than dividing gun owners into good guys and bad guys and arguing that all we have to do is keep the bad guys from owning guns, the policies they have implemented—the ones described in the table above—ensure that fewer guns are available and that they're harder for anyone to get. Comprehensive background checks, licensing, and safety training all work because they make it harder for people to obtain weapons in the first place and significantly reduce the probability that they will use those weapons to kill themselves or each other.

It is the very same approach that successfully reduced injuries and deaths in motor vehicles (that other symbol of masculinity and freedom). For the first half of the twentieth century, "the traffic safety establishment perpetuated the belief that drivers were responsible for accidents. . . . Drivers were suspect, while the actions of engineers and automakers were unquestioned. [The proposed remedies] dealt with eliminating driver fault."[6] The motor industry was in denial, with slogans like "It's the nut behind the wheel." Its leaders argued that all we had to do was educate people to become better drivers. In the second half of the twentieth century, thanks to the persistent factualism of doctors and scientists, we changed our approach. As a country, we stopped blaming drivers for their deaths and instead established speed limits, installed lighting on our roads, greatly improved the safety features in cars, and tightened the standards one must meet to become a driver. David Hemenway, a public health researcher at Harvard, writes in his classic *Private Guns, Public Health*, "It is, after all, often easier to change the behavior of a few corporate executives at one point in time than that of two hundred million drivers on a daily basis."

The same logic has to apply to guns. It is far more efficient (and effective!) to pass reforms that regulate the firearm industry, mandating that these deadly weapons are manufactured with mandatory safety features, for instance, and raising the bar for gun ownership, than it is to change the behavior of millions of people once they already have guns in their hands.

The successes of other countries can guide America to reduce its high levels of gun homicides, suicides, and accidental shootings. The timing of those reforms also offers a hint as to what it will take for the United States to reach its own tipping point and implement the reforms that have already saved so many lives elsewhere.

How can we push our lawmakers to dramatically change their approach to guns? If global experience is any indicator, it will take a combination of Americans demanding change, shaming lawmakers who remain beholden to the NRA, and pushing them to place the interests of their constituents ahead of the financial and political needs of powerful special interests. A single brave politician who can publicly break ties with the NRA and advance bold priorities could become a tipping point to a new—and much more sane—approach to gun policy. "What could happen in the United States is what happened here in Australia, which is a reversal in attitude toward people who own firearms and a realization that you need to treat this just as seriously as the road toll," Alpers, the Australian gun researcher, told me when I asked him how he saw America solving its gun problem. "Thirty thousand people killed by firearms is a hell of a lot of people, and it will take a determination that will have to be raised [like that] around the road toll, the tobacco disease control, and of course HIV."

In the chapters that follow, I lay out a road map for driving that determination to achieve real change and implement the policies outlined in the Compact.

Gun Owners Support a World with Fewer Guns

One of the best ways to create change is by educating those around you, but in this case, some of the hardest sells may be gun owners. Sometimes, however, they will surprise you.

"When I go to a public gun range, I am horrified in the way that a race car driver is scared on the highway," Sam told me when I asked him to describe the vast majority of the people who own guns in America. "They do not have a fucking clue what they're doing, and it's horribly scary," he said.

While I anxiously arranged my travel to the two-day firearm training course in the Southwest, I connected with other gun owners who, like Sam, felt misunderstood, frustrated, underappreciated—caricatured, even. They slowly reshaped my understanding of what it means to own a firearm in America, painting a far more colorful and intricate picture of American gun ownership than the rigidly divided political debate does.

"Many gun owners are just big freaking nerds. It is just another thing to nerd out about," Eryn Sepp, a white thirty-year-old Iraq War veteran who once worked at a gun range, told me over a lunch of milk and strawberry shortcake. Her blue eyes sparkled as she described what appealed to her about owning firearms. "I mean, if it's not World of Warcraft and it's not Pokemon Go, it's guns," she said. "People like to be excited about something. They like to feel like they know the terminology. There is this culture you get accepted in the more you can talk the language. 'I mean, gosh, if you've ever fired a .17 HMR, then are you just not the coolest? What a rare round!'" she said enthusiastically, throwing her head back in laughter. "It's fun. It's just fun to know about these things." (That's a .17 caliber Hornady Magnum Rimfire cartridge, by the way, a smaller-caliber projectile in a necked down .22 magnum casing made to achieve greater muzzle velocity and a flatter trajectory than previously available in a rimfire rifle.)

For Eryn, guns are a sport and a means of self-expression. She talked about her craft and her firearms like a musician showing off a 1960 Gibson Les Paul Sunburst. Sam struck a similar tone. He first encountered what he refers to as real, authentic, hardcore gun enthusiasts at the elite gun training facility he had invited me to experience for myself—an institute that has helped develop and establish the shooting and safety techniques that have been adopted by law enforcement and militaries all over the world.

Sam set foot in the center after coming home from his second tour of duty in Iraq, frustrated by the U.S. military's limited firearm training options. The experience transformed his entire life. He dived into a new world inhabited by about a million or so truly dedicated gun enthusiasts he describes as the real "regulated militia." This loose group of Americans travel around the country taking weeklong courses in guns, marksmanship, and any other firearm-related subject you can imagine, ultimately receiving better training than the military or the police. They're a varied lot—orthopedic surgeons, truck drivers, teachers—but they share the common values of responsibility: "responsibility for their personal security and responsibility to own and use guns in the best possible way, by investing in training and practice," Sam said, adding that these gun users strive to live "a lifestyle of the modern minutemen, who exist to support and augment the police/military/government in order to fully manifest our values and lifestyle choices." He joked that "for most of us, Lady Gaga said it best: 'We were born this way.'"

Sam and Eryn see guns as an expression (or enhancement) of the lifestyle they choose to live. Maj Toure believes he needs firearms to survive. Maj is an African American man around my age from Philadelphia. In his North Philly neighborhood, residents inevitably come into contact with guns, whether they like it or not, and do not have access to the kind of gun courses Sam does. "A lot of times in my community, firearms are available before you have the information to even handle them properly. You can run across a gun at fifteen," the dreadlocked artist and activist told *The Trace*.[1]

Maj is an activist, a Republican, and an NRA member and he is building a movement to educate and train African Americans to properly use firearms. His organization, Black Guns Matter, holds trainings and informational sessions around the country about how to shoot firearms and legally carry them. "What we want to do is, if anyone runs across a gun at a young age, we want them to know what to do and not to do. It's about making sure people from my demographic aren't doing the wrong thing." Or are perceived as doing the wrong thing by the police. "What we're trying to do is say that just because you have a gun does not make you the bad guy. But while you have your firearm, which you have the right to have, you have to be a responsible, card-carrying good guy." Maj argues that by teaching people conflict-management skills and using guns only when they absolutely have to, many communities of color will be safer—and law enforcement will view armed black men as less of a threat.

Using a gun for self-defense is rare. Surveys show that in America a gun is used defensively in about one out of every hundred crimes of personal contact. There are an estimated eighty thousand defensive gun uses in the United States per year.

Eryn is responsible for one of those uses. About five years ago, she was sitting in the parking lot of a hotel on her way to a Black Eyed Peas concert. Suddenly a man came up to her car window and threatened to rob her, demanding she empty her wallet. Reflexively, Eryn grabbed her unloaded Kimber .45, which just happened to be sitting on the armrest between the driver and passenger seats, stuck it in the man's face, and yelled, "Get the fuck away from me." The attacker bolted, but the incident shook Eryn and reinforced her habit of constantly scanning for threats. It is a quality she picked up even before joining the military, and she felt good that at that moment, in that car, she was armed, even though not loaded. "My fear for my personal safety comes from going about my daily life as a woman. I heard an author say once that you could tell from twenty-five meters away if a guy is going to say something smart to you, and that is absolutely true. Walking down the street, you know if some guy is going to try something. I think every woman goes through her life like that, and so then you give a woman a gun and you have given her power back, and I think that is why a lot of women like to shoot."

The tension between, on the one hand, building communities with fewer guns and fewer gun crimes and, on the other, the desire to own a firearm for self-protection—for *you* would never use it irresponsibly!—is a sticking point. It helps explain why this work is so difficult. Many people recognize that, yes, we have so many guns and they're too easy to get, *but* guns are also superb for self-defense in certain circumstances. Eryn and millions of other women would be safer if America had far fewer guns. The robber would've been less likely to have been carrying a gun himself. Still, statistics and probability are worthless in the moment of threat. This contradiction is perhaps the central challenge for gun control advocates.

Gun owners like Sam are living out what they describe as their "martial values" of self-sacrifice for the protection of others, and those like Eryn are carrying for their own protection. They are not responsible for America's gun problem. For the most part, they are well trained in how and when to fire a gun, and they have proven that they can own guns responsibly. Even Maj preaches safe gun ownership and is working to minimize actual gun use.

On the other side are the millions and millions of people who buy weapons out of fear, blindly rushing out to purchase firearms anytime a politician floats new gun-safety regulations. For many of them, gun ownership is less about protection and more an expression of a social identity purposely constructed—as we've seen—by the NRA.

"They say, 'It's my right,' yet do nothing in the realm of responsibility," Sam complained. "They want to own guns because it gives them a false sense of security, a weak sense of power, and with it they talk about overthrowing the government. These are the people who bring AR-15s to Starbucks and open-carry pistols in order to make people uncomfortable and challenge the police. These are the people who are ignorant, incompetent, do not train, and give people like me a bad name."

Eryn goes shooting at a gun range with her fiancé at least once a month and encounters many such people there. She is always careful to avoid talk about her support for Democratic politicians and other topics that would betray her progressive leanings. "I joined the NRA because I came home from Iraq and I started working at a gun range, so of course it would make sense that the NRA was going to be my people," she said. "But what I did not realize when I joined was that there are two different NRAs. There's the NRA that's really great and does education in the communities, but then there's the NRA-ILA [the group's lobbying arm, the Institute for Legislative Action], and I did *not* understand I was getting into *that* organization when I joined the NRA."

How You Can Build a Future
with Fewer Guns

With this book I aim to establish a bold long-term objective for the gun control movement that will actually solve the crisis we face. That goal? Moving us toward a world with fewer guns and embracing the kind of policies that go after the guns themselves—policies that have successfully reduced gun deaths in other parts of the world.

I understand that this cannot be achieved in a day, a week, or a month—but that's exactly the point. I want us to break out of the habit of focusing on what is practically possible today and instead establish a clear goal for the future. Let's think beyond a set of policies and ask ourselves: What does winning on this issue actually look like? What kind of country do we want to build together?

To me, and to a majority of Americans, winning is a future with significantly fewer guns in circulation, in which guns are significantly harder to get and gun owners have to meet high training standards.

Like any social movement, achieving such a bold goal will require a lot of hard work, a lot of organizing and determination.

Most important, it will require a diverse movement with many different people and various strategies, approaches, campaigns, and methodologies—litigation, legislation, public education, direct action, electoral work, state-based work, and group organizing.

The different voices in the movement won't always agree and they may not even share all of the goals laid out in these pages. Gun violence has a different impact in different communities. To be successful, the various groups will have to work in a coordinated fashion to help each other succeed, but much more important than the success of any individual campaign or strategy is the ability of the movement as a whole to stay on track toward its ultimate goal. No one person, no one approach, no one strategy, no one victory is going to be able to deliver on the goal all by itself. That's just not how social movements work, and it's not how political change actually happens.

In this chapter, I envision a way to reach the goal of fewer guns in safer communities. It explains the role I play in that movement and the role I think you can play as well.

Because movements are complex organisms with many moving parts and pieces, when I first co-founded Guns Down America in the aftermath of the shooting at the Pulse nightclub in Orlando, Florida, I did so because I thought I could add something the movement was missing.

In 2016, we had organizations that focused on crafting the policy we needed to help reduce gun violence. The Center for American Progress, where I've spent most of my career, is one example. We also had organizations that focused on driving policy and advocacy in the states, and others that played the insider game in Washington, DC, lobbying members of Congress to pass legislation like universal background checks and organizing campaigns to fight measures the NRA promoted. We even had voices that acted as NRA watchdogs, reporting on the ways it was recruiting members and building closer ties to gun manufacturers and dealers.

However, there was no group that was actively working to reclaim the narrative from the gun lobby, to set out a bold goal for the movement and work day and night to insert it into our national conversation. In other words, we had no equivalent of PETA or Greenpeace, two organizations that are unapologetically bold in both tactics and asks.

In my view, these kind of groups play a critical role in any social movement. They broaden the public conversation about the issue from piecemeal incremental changes to big bold goals and, in the process, provide the space for other voices—that play different roles—within the movement to cut deals, pass bills, and seek changes that will be stronger and bolder than if the conversation had remained limited.

The gun rights side of the debate and its players do function this way. While the NRA is the largest and most influential gun lobby in the nation, it is far from the most radical. Smaller groups, like the Gun Owners of America, the Second Amendment Foundation, and the Citizens Committee for the Right to Keep and Bear Arms, operate in the NRA's shadow, but they all play a critical role in pushing the NRA to stay true to the movement's "guns everywhere and for everyone" goals.

Here is a perfect example.

Back in 2013, in the aftermath of the shooting in Newtown, Connecticut, which left twenty-six people dead, including twenty children, lawmakers from both sides of the aisle believed that the horror of dead first-graders would force the country to tighten its loose gun laws and at least require almost all individuals buying a gun to pass an instant background check. An overwhelming majority of Americans supported such reform, and a bipartisan duo of fairly conservative senators, Joe Manchin and Patrick Toomey, began working on legislative language that could pass a Republican-controlled Congress.

Initially, lawmakers from both parties were very optimistic. Staffers on Capitol Hill even told me conservative members would privately assure their more progressive colleagues that they could see themselves voting for such a measure. Even the NRA came to the table. It began offering guidance about the language and provisions it could potentially live with—maybe not actively support or endorse, but at least tolerate.

But then everything changed.

More radical gun rights organizations, like the Gun Owners of America, got wind of the NRA's tacit support and sprang into action. They began sending out fund-raising letters characterizing the powerful lobby as a sellout that had gone soft, each proclaiming itself the one true defender of gun rights.

Never one to be outflanked, the NRA pulled back its conversations with lawmakers on the Hill and turned against the Manchin-Toomey background-check bill. It argued that lawmakers should address problems in the existing background-check system and do more to encourage states to send records into it, insisted the proposed legislation would lead to a national gun registry and pave the way for firearm confiscation. The Senate ultimately defeated the measure in a vote of 54–46.[1] It needed 60 votes to advance.

In a movement dedicated to expanding gun ownership and defeating any restrictions on guns, the furthest right wing of the movement plays a critical role: it keeps the gun rights movement true to its goals by staking out an uncompromising position—no gun regulations, no way—and successfully pulling the NRA toward it.

The gun violence prevention movement has no equivalent dynamic and, as a result, we lack the clear and bold goal that the other side possesses and the grassroots energy and excitement to achieve it. We have failed to tap into the values, energy, and excitement of the American people and have been unable to invite people to stay with the work over the long term.

I established Guns Down America to help provide a hopeful, bigger vision for those of us working to reduce gun violence. We are not interested in talking about piecemeal solutions—universal background checks, closing loopholes in existing laws, and so on. We're trying to articulate a clear, unified goal of building a future with fewer guns and developing a strategy for getting us there.

It is a goal I hope the rest of the movement will adopt. But we are a diverse movement; so long as we coordinate our efforts and support each other, we will all be able to move in the same direction together. Not everyone may agree with our goal, but we don't need everyone. We just need enough people to join our cause and help us push forward; enough lawmakers from relatively progressive states, like Massachusetts or New York, where some of the reforms I propose are already a reality, to champion these policies on the national stage; and enough bold leaders with national ambitions to stake out a strong goal, build popular support among people who have had enough of the mass shootings, suicides, and everyday gun violence that are ravaging our communities, and thus pull our national conversation toward real reforms. We've seen similar shifts in the health care debate, the minimum wage and economic inequality debate, the LGBT equality debate; it's time to apply the same approach to the gun debate.

You are probably asking, okay, Igor, what's your strategy? What can each of us do to reach that goal—especially in the face of such well-funded opposition and lawmakers who continue to ignore the will of their constituents in order to advance their political careers? I am asked this question everywhere I go, and if I'm being honest, I say that there is no easy, simple answer. If there were, we would have solved this problem a long time ago.

Nevertheless, there is also no reason to get discouraged. Social movements of the past have accomplished big things, but only if they had a clear goal and an accessible strategy that other people could understand and find a way to contribute to.

Learning from the Fight for Marriage Equality

If there exists a major social movement in America that has established a clear long-term goal and then, over a period of decades, developed a multi-pronged strategy and achieved it, I can think of no better example than the successful push for marriage equality.

I covered LGBTQ issues for *ThinkProgress* during the Obama years and witnessed firsthand the decades of work come to fruition. Still, in order to understand the movement and the lessons it could hold for building a future with fewer guns, I had to talk to the "godfather of gay marriage."[1]

Evan Wolfson did not invent the idea of marriage equality. Gay and lesbian couples began asking state and federal courts for the freedom to marry several years after the riots at the Stonewall Inn in Manhattan in June 1969. Wolfson was the first to argue, in 1983, that those courts that had rejected it were wrong, then resurrect the goal and lay out a clear long-term strategy for how to get there. Over the next thirty years, he advocated for marriage equality within the broader LGBT movement and built the critical mass necessary for it to become reality.

When Wolfson first laid out his vision in a law school thesis, he argued that marriage equality was both a goal and a strategy. It was a goal because it would provide gay and lesbian couples with all of the rights, benefits, and responsibilities of marriage; it was a strategy because it would lead to greater acceptance of gay and lesbian people generally by changing how straight people view them.

"When I put this forward, there was significant dismay, disagreement, disbelief, not only within the world at large, but even within the movement," Wolfson told me on the phone in the summer of 2018. His fellow "band of warriors" systematically rejected or contested his arguments for the next ten years. Some argued that marriage was a bad goal because it was a failed patriarchal institution! Others maintained that the movement should not be fighting to assimilate; it should instead be inventing its own relationships and redefining the structure of family. Others still contended that fighting for marriage was too difficult, premature, and could even trigger a conservative response that would set the movement for gay civil rights back decades.

Still, Wolfson persisted as a self-described "internal gadfly" during much of the 1980s and 1990s. Throughout this period he worked to convince those around him that setting out a bold goal like freedom to marry would prove more effective than simply calling for more public acceptance of same-sex couples and less discrimination against them.

"You should ask for what you want and not bargain against yourself. You may leave the negotiation or the round or the battle taking less than you initially wanted. But you should not go in asking for less than you want," he told me. In other words, you won't get half a loaf of bread by asking for half a loaf. You have to ask for the whole loaf.

That principle has long guided my own advocacy in gun violence prevention. When I formed Guns Down America, I realized that no other group was asking for what all of us believed was necessary to truly reduce gun violence: fewer guns. As a result, we were not having much success on the legislative front getting the policies we believed we needed, and we are not building a strong people-powered movement that people can buy into. We are not offering bold solutions that people believe will succeed in reducing gun violence.

Along with lack of a clear goal, the gun control movement has also lacked a clear strategy.

A tight strategy is essential, Wolfson told me. It tells you exactly what you have to do and what you do not have to do. It ensures that you are not distracted by other obligations, educates everyday Americans about how you are achieving your goal, and allows them to plug into it. A clear strategy also helps sustain you through the inevitable turmoil of a movement: the wins, the losses, and everything in between.

The marriage movement reminds us that after you've focused on one long-term objective, incremental changes that move you closer to your goal are essential building blocks to achieving your success, just as every yard forward moves a football team a little closer to the goalposts. Each gain provides a motivating victory for advocates in all parts of the movement and shows that progress is indeed possible. As the wins accumulate, they accustom the general public to accepting gains on the issue and, just as important, permit advocates to demonstrate the insufficiency of half measures, redoubling efforts toward the ultimate goal.

Wolfson faced an important movement-defining decision after achieving incremental success in 2000, when Vermont recognized gay and lesbian civil unions but not marriage.

Should he accept the half measure or reject it? Would accepting it signal to others that the fight was over and suck energy out of the struggle to full marriage equality? Maybe people would think that civil unions were good enough. After much debate and deliberation, Wolfson decided to accept the win—but then push for more later.

He went on to argue that because the sky didn't fall when gay and lesbian couples entered into civil unions, why deny them access to the institution of marriage? And why have two different names for the same thing? Wolfson began to disparage civil unions and argue that they were not an adequate substitute for marriage because they were fundamentally unequal.

The fight toward the long-term goal was very much still on.

"What we needed in the late nineties was the affirmation of gay couples at the marital level," Wolfson told me in describing his dual strategy. "And then what we needed later was the insufficiency of civil union as a substitute for marriage itself."

The most substantial wave of change that helped pave the way for marriage equality took place during President Obama's presidency. Gays, lesbians, and bisexuals were permitted to serve openly in the armed forces through the repeal of Don't Ask, Don't Tell. The administration stopped defending the Defense of Marriage Act (DOMA), which defined marriage as a union between a man and a woman for the purposes of federal programs. Obama himself came out in support of marriage equality, and ultimately the Supreme Court found that preventing gays and lesbians from entering into equal marriage was unconstitutional.

All of that happened as a result of the foundation Wolfson and other advocates had laid down over the preceding decades of hard, often thankless, focused advocacy toward the goal of marriage equality. By the time Obama was sworn in as president, Wolfson was no longer a gadfly; his goal had become a goal of most grassroots LGBT advocates, and throughout the Obama era they pushed a reluctant White House to act on its equality agenda.

While reporting for *ThinkProgress*, I covered gay and lesbian service members who tied themselves to the White House fence demanding equal service and rejecting the politics of incremental change. I covered grassroots advocates who criticized the president for initially defending DOMA and for not coming out for marriage early enough. They wanted change now and could not care less about the political process in Washington.

As I wrote these articles, established political operatives and Democrats would tell me these grassroots actions were disruptive, naive, or, worse yet, counterproductive. The president, they argued, had to be sensitive to political realities. He was on the right side, they told me, but he needed time to make these decisions so as to avoid political backlash. Acting too swiftly could set back the movement and undo the progress already made.

It's easy, in hindsight, to laugh at these voices or view their stance as a miscalculation of the winds of political change. A sober reading of the history, however, suggests that they were as necessary for progress as Wolfson and the grassroots groups that were pushing the administration to boldly embrace true equality.

Journalist Kerry Eleveld, who covered the progress LGBT Americans made during the Obama presidency with inspiring persistency and intelligence, told me that, in the end, "everybody ended up being right to some extent."

Take Don't Ask, Don't Tell. On the campaign trail, President Obama had pledged to repeal the discriminatory law, but almost two years into his administration, it remained on the books, and Democrats in Congress were not rushing to get rid of it after losing their congressional majority in the 2010 midterm elections.

Knowing that the window of opportunity was closing fast, grassroots advocates clamored for action, engaging in protests and direct actions and shaming lawmakers for doing nothing, while the insiders were preaching caution and patience. With just days left until a new Republican-controlled House would come into power, Congress added the repeal measure to a must-pass bill, and Obama signed it into law in December 2010.

Here, too, diverse voices were necessary for achieving progress.

Eleveld, author of *Don't Tell Me to Wait: How the Fight for Gay Rights Changed America and Transformed Obama's Presidency*, told me, "Don't Ask, Don't Tell repeal would not have gotten across the finish

line if there weren't people who knew Capitol Hill really well and
could get the ear of very prominent lawmakers in positions of power
within the last month of that Congress. But it also would not have
gotten to that point if the grassroots activists hadn't been pushing
for it all along."

In other words, everybody had a role to play, and a sort of righteous cycle emerged. The grassroots activists pushed the professional
political insiders to expect more, not to settle for middling progress,
but the movement would not have progressed to that point had the
professional advocates and insiders not laid the groundwork that ripened the issue for action. A successful movement is a cacophony of
voices, not a fine-tuned choir.

Another similarity between the gun control movement and the
fight for LGBT equality is familiarity of experience.

For decades science had been disproving and professional psychology had been gradually abandoning the idea that nonstandard
sexuality was some sort of disease rather than an array of natural
and normal variations along the whole sexual spectrum in humans
(and most other animals). But it took a long time for this view to
spread more widely. One of the factors that helped drive the general
population toward accepting and supporting marriage equality was
the coming out of gay people themselves, a wave that really began
during the AIDS crisis of the 1980s, when the community realized
that silence would lead to death. It was a process that even a visionary
like Wolfson could not have predicted, but in the ensuing decades, a
growing number of Americans' family members, friends, and neighbors told their loved ones that they were gay, lesbian, bisexual, or
transgender. The general population began to see gays and lesbians
of every religion, every race, and both genders as human beings,
rather than caricatures who could be demonized as deviants who
didn't deserve civil rights.

A growing number of families now saw themselves as part of the push for marriage equality. Heterosexuals began to see themselves as part of the movement for the sake of people they loved—their families, friends, neighbors, and community members.

A similar phenomenon has led to gradual deprohibition of cannabis, and the same thing could now be happening with guns. As gun manufacturers pump more and more guns into our communities, more and more people of all races, genders, religions, and socioeconomic levels are dying from or living with horrific gun injuries.

The coverage of mass shootings and our ritualized grief after them continue to educate people about the dangers of too many guns. We all see ourselves in the faces of the bereaved, and we imagine photos of our own loved ones posted at the candlelit memorial.

That dynamic of familiarity allowed the LGBT equality movement to achieve its goal faster than anyone could have predicted. If we build our movement and pair it with successful strategies, we can start moving toward a future with fewer guns sooner rather than later.

A Strategy for Building a
World with Fewer Guns

In this book I propose a clear goal for the gun control movement: fewer guns. One way to reach that goal is by weakening the NRA financially in order to significantly hamper its ability to buy off "thoughts and prayers" lawmakers, intimidate politicians, and block legislative progress. As the NRA continues to bleed resources, lawmakers will be more willing to introduce the bold reforms outlined in the Compact and will be more likely to vote for them, too.

Guns Down America kept this strategy front of mind in the fall of 2017 when the NRA began marketing a new insurance policy called Carry Guard. The program, aimed at the NRA's mostly white membership, provided insurance coverage to those who shoot someone with a gun. It offered up to $250,000 in immediate payments for criminal defense, "cleanup costs," a replacement firearm, bail, bonds, and psychological support. The policies, which ranged in cost from $14 to $49 a month, were administered by Lockton Affinity and insured by Chubb, two of the world's largest publicly traded property and casualty insurance companies.

The NRA's marketing of the policies was particularly grotesque. Its ads warned members that they faced a violent threat around every corner and needed not only a gun, but also an insurance policy to protect them when they, as they would inevitably have to, discharged their weapons against—you guessed it!—a black or brown criminal. The policies played on the same racist stereotypes the NRA's leaders spouted on a regular basis and the racial tensions it exploited in order to grow its membership.

Worse, Carry Guard could also be seen as an expansion of the deadly stand-your-ground laws the NRA had promoted throughout the country, laws that disproportionately harm communities of color by letting whites shoot blacks and claim self-defense. My friend the policy analyst Chelsea Parsons had studied these laws and found that they not only lead to an increase in state homicide rates, but also have a racially disparate impact. She found that more than 35 percent of shootings involving a white person with a gun and a black victim are found to be justified under the law, but less than 4 percent of cases involving a black shooter and white victim were categorized in the same way.[1]

Carry Guard was not only morally reprehensible and conducive to a higher rate of gun deaths, but it was also making a lot of money for the NRA. We talked about launching a public education campaign against the insurers who were offering the policies. Our ask of them was simple: break ties with the NRA and stop contributing to gun violence among underserved communities.

The campaign fed into our larger goal of building a future of fewer guns. The NRA profited from selling these insurance products, profits that would be turned into political donations that would push lawmakers to embrace "guns everywhere and for everyone." Furthermore, it was consistent with our strategy of weakening the gun lobby by undermining its relationships with large American corporations.

As we began drafting the letters to the CEOs of both insurers, we also commissioned research to learn more about the product and company management, seeking an entry point into the corporate leadership.

We needed partners in this effort, particularly those who represented members of the African American community, which stood to suffer disproportionately from the NRA's new product.

I immediately contacted Rashad Robinson of Color of Change, an online organization with over a million members that pressures corporations to "create a more human and less hostile world for Black people in America."

In 2011, Color of Change successfully forced over one hundred large corporations to break ties with the American Legislative Exchange Council (ALEC), a conservative association that, among many other unjust policies, drafted and helped pass legislation to suppress the black vote. Color of Change had found success in pushing companies to change in the past, and I understood that its wisdom and guidance would prove essential to our campaign. The organization agreed to partner with us, and as we drafted our letter to Chubb and Lockton, it wrote its own, educating the two insurers about the dangers of their business arrangement and announcing a public campaign to expose it.

Having sent those letters, I embarked on another mission: getting Sybrina Fulton, the mother of Trayvon Martin, to serve as the public face of our campaign. When I first learned of the Carry Guard policy, Martin's tragic killing popped into my head. The unarmed seventeen-year-old was shot and killed while visiting relatives in Florida, the first state to enact a stand-your-ground law. What if Martin's killer, George Zimmerman, had had Carry Guard insurance? Providing him with financial assistance as Martin's family grieved the loss of a son, it could only have promoted his "shoot first, ask questions later" mentality. Zimmerman was acquitted of murdering Trayvon on grounds of self-defense. Even his lawyers did not seek immunity under the state's stand-your-ground law, but the judge in the case referenced the law when he instructed the jury that Zimmerman had had no duty to retreat and could use deadly force if he felt it was necessary to defend himself.

Someone on our team had a connection to the Trayvon Martin Foundation, which the family established in the aftermath of his death, and Fulton agreed to participate and serve as the spokesperson for the push. She recorded an emotional video message calling on the insurance companies behind the NRA's Carry Guard to drop the program, which could have provided up to $1.5 million to Zimmerman.

"Tell the two insurance companies, Chubb and Lockton Affinity, who created NRA Carry Guard, that you know who they are," Fulton said in our ad. "Tell them . . . that if they keep offering murder insurance . . . they'll never get your business. Tell them they should be ashamed to do the bidding of the gun lobby."

The ad ended with two powerful sentences that give me chills every time I watch the spot. "My name is Sybrina Fulton, and my son's name was Trayvon Martin," Fulton says, looking directly into the camera. "I'm an American, and it's time to put the guns down."

We sent the ad to our email list and Color of Change sent it to theirs. We blasted it through social media, previewed it to the press, and offered people a way to plug in, urging them to sign our petition demanding that Chubb and Lockton end the relationship.

The campaign took off.

We earned tons of national and local press coverage and garnered hundreds of thousands of signatures. Even the NRA took note, characterizing our campaign as "stupid." Soon, Everytown for Gun Safety got involved. Regulators in New York began investigating the business arrangement behind the product. Ultimately they banned the program from the state and imposed a $7 million fine on Lockton and one of $1.3 million on Chubb. Other states are considering doing the same.

We later found out that, just weeks after we launched our campaign, Chubb quietly told the NRA that it would not be renewing its contract with the lobby. Lockton soon followed suit, pulling out of the effort in the aftermath of the shooting in Parkland, Florida, right after we hired an airplane to fly over its headquarters urging it to drop the program. We alerted the press about the maneuver to make sure more people saw it. The idea of flying the airplane came after several billboard companies around Lockton headquarters prevented us from purchasing billboard space calling out Lockton by name. We had hoped to publicly shame the company in its own community and build support among its employees, who could advocate for our cause from the inside. Turned out, the flyover worked just as well.

The Carry Guard effort became one of Guns Down America's most successful corporate campaigns. In the summer of 2018, the NRA filed court papers claiming it was in grave financial jeopardy and could soon "be unable to exist." Andrew Cuomo, the governor of New York, also warned New York banks and other major corporations about doing business with the gun lobby and urged other governors to do the same. The lobby publicly claimed that this move, combined with the loss it was feeling from the end of the Carry Guard program, was taking a financial toll.

Bleeding the NRA dry will require more successful campaigns. An organization that takes in $160 to $415 million every single year will not change after losing corporate sponsorships. (Technically, only $30 million is earmarked for lobbying.) But corporations throughout the country are starting to realize that doing business with the NRA and supporting gunmakers and guns is toxic; it could tarnish a company's most valuable asset, its brand. They simply do not want to be associated with firearms. They fear the possibility that they could be held liable for helping a shooter easily access a gun—particularly in the court of public opinion.

In the summer of 2018, after Trump allowed blueprints for 3-D-printed guns to be posted online for anybody to download and print using a 3-D printer, corporations took voluntary action to ensure that their technology could not be used in such a way. Sculpteo, a major 3-D printing company, banned firearm printing. Another, Materialise, is developing technology to prevent the production of guns.[2] Even tech giants like Facebook have blocked individuals from posting 3-D gun blueprints on their social media platforms.[3]

The overwhelming majority of Americans reject the NRA's "guns everywhere" agenda and its practice of hijacking our democracy by buying off politicians. At least twenty-eight companies have broken ties with the NRA since the shooting in Parkland, Florida, and, given where public opinion is headed, corporations will not want to be associated with the gun lobby for long. Especially if we continue to pressure them.

We Will Win

I know a secret the gun lobby does not want you to know: the demographic trends taking place in our country today will make it far harder for the NRA and gun extremists to continue hijacking our democracy and stalling progress toward gun reform in the future.

As of 2016, just 32 percent of American households owned firearms. In the 1970s, that number hovered around 50 percent. Gun ownership is falling fast as the United States continues to urbanize and Americans are turning to other forms of recreation.[1] Non-gun-owning households make up the overwhelming majority of American citizens and—if they organize around this issue—they can put it to rest for good by electing politicians who will enact the provisions included in the Compact and build a future with fewer guns and fewer gun deaths.

The people are already ahead of the politicians on this issue. In the summer of 2018, Guns Down America commissioned a poll to figure out where Americans stood on the bold ideas we advocate. It turns out that 59 percent of Americans back building a future with fewer guns—even without any prominent lawmakers publicly campaigning for it! Americans have long been on the right side of this issue, but we have lacked political leaders willing to transform these beliefs into reality.

Our poll found that overwhelming majorities of Democrats *and* Republicans support the policy solutions this book puts forward:

- 79 percent favor a voluntary government buyback program
- 78 percent support banning assault weapons
- 89 percent believe a license should be required to purchase a handgun

Support will only continue to grow as the country grapples with a growing number of mass shootings. Americans throughout the country will continue to rise up against the gun lobby and the politicians who support it. The fight for marriage equality taught us that the gap between public opinion and political leadership can remain wide for only so long. Politicians are risk-averse, but they respond to organized public pressure. When they are confronted by their voters or when they see an opportunity, triggered by an event or whatever else, to close that gap, they do.

The new energy surrounding the student activists from Parkland, Florida, is just such an opportunity. The Parkland students transformed their grief into energy, into forward-looking action. As a result, in the five months following the shooting, governors in twenty-six states signed fifty-five bills aimed at reducing gun violence; fifteen of the governors were Republicans. These reforms included laws preventing domestic abusers from obtaining firearms, banning bump stocks, tightening state-based concealed-carry requirements, and increasing funding for community-based crime intervention programs. Over the same period, advocates defeated forty-four NRA-backed bills.[2]

The Parkland students spoke with authenticity and raw emotion. They had spent their school lives practicing active-shooter drills and had just witnessed seventeen of their fellow classmates and school staff gunned down with an assault weapon. They had no use for the caution or talking points that lawmakers often use when discussing guns. You didn't hear a lot about the Second Amendment or responsible gun owners. Little of that NRA-based framing entered the conversation in the weeks immediately following the Parkland shooting.

That's why their message resonated. It was real, unrehearsed, and urgent. They were marching for their lives.

They had a problem with the fact that a student was easily able to obtain a weapon of war, walk into their school, and shoot thirty-four of their classmates and teachers in six minutes—despite numerous warnings to authorities that he threatened to do so. He was able to do that because the NRA had spent millions of dollars buying off politicians to ensure that restrictions on such weapons could never become law. Guns and their accessibility were precisely the problem, and the students actively confronted their lawmakers about it without any of the expected niceties.

I cheered wildly as I watched the CNN town hall from Parkland, Florida, in the week following the Valentine's Day 2018 shooting. On the stage, seated across from the most vocal student Parkland survivors were Representative Ted Deutch and Senator Marco Rubio. Rubio had taken some $10,000 from the NRA. The audience and the students challenged Rubio to explain why weapons designed for the battlefield could be legally purchased in most states in America. He fumbled, stumbled, and then threw out some talking point about how it would be difficult to design a law that bans "assault weapons" without going after broader classes of semiautomatic firearms. "Then ban them all," the crowd yelled.

Americans, I realized, have long favored the goal of fewer guns and safer communities. They just haven't had leaders with the courage to support it. The months after the Parkland shooting felt different because the students had infused the issue and the movement with a new hopeful energy not bound by immediate political realities or vote counts. They gave us hope because they defined winning as taking our country back from the gun lobby. They had our complete attention.

All of us must play our part and lean into whatever we're good at, whatever value we bring to the table, to help build a future with fewer guns. For some of us, that may be following gun violence prevention groups on social media, calling members of Congress, confronting them during a campaign stop or a town hall event, organizing a rally or a die-in at a public place (or, better yet, at all of the members' district offices!), or educating our friends and neighbors about the consequences of our horrific gun laws.

Our action should not be confined to the federal government. Most gun laws are made on the state level, and those lawmakers rarely find themselves the targets of focused advocacy. Call their offices, stage actions at the state capitol, bombard their Facebook and Twitter pages with your demand. If it embarrasses them for acting like NRA puppets, then all the better.

Each one of us is a change agent. Change will come through a million small actions. It's up to us to take them.

ACKNOWLEDGMENTS

I've been putting off writing this part of the book for fear of forgetting someone or, more accurately, failing to adequately recognize all of the people who have made it possible for me to start, write, and ultimately complete this project. And now, after months of procrastination and anxiety, as I wake up early on a Sunday and head into my WeWork office to write these words, I find myself sitting across from a flex space co-worker wearing a bright orange NRA hat. (If there's a lesson in there somewhere, I'm not sure what it is, though I'm now confident there's no escaping our trolling culture.)

That being said, this book would not have been possible without the stewardship, mentorship, and encouragement of so many people.

First and foremost, I have to thank Chelsea Parsons of the Center for American Progress (CAP). Chelsea's contribution to the gun violence prevention movement is immeasurable. She both crafts the policies that shape our movement and articulates those ideas in the clearest terms possible. Chelsea is the fiercest of policy wonks *and* advocates. Chelsea has taught me (almost) everything I know about guns and I am so grateful for all of the time she spent helping me form the arguments in this book and reviewing its different components—from the initial book proposal I put together in 2016 to the final version of the Second Amendment Compact contained within it. When I first started this project Chelsea and I were work colleagues, and we have since become good friends. I am so grateful for that friendship.

There are so many other people at CAP who believed in me throughout my ten years there and who gave me the courage to think that I could even take on such an ambitious project. They include John Podesta, who would bring me into meetings I had no place being in when I first started at CAP as a young health care reporter; Faiz Shakir and Judd Legum, who gave me such amazing opportunities to advance at ThinkProgress; Neera Tanden, who after the 2016 election inspired me to continue working in progressive politics; and, of course, my dear friend Angie Kelley.

Angie believed in me when I didn't believe in myself. She taught me how to think strategically about problems, identify our goals, and channel all of our resources toward meeting them. She showed me how to run a meeting, manage people, solve complex problems, act and think like a leader. I still can't accomplish any of this with a tenth of Angie's grace or strength, but thankfully our lessons continue to this day.

(My NRA-hat-wearing co-worker left as I was writing that last part, so thankfully he did not see me tear up—repeatedly.)

The team at Guns Down America has supported me every step of the way, particularly Stephen Geer, who lit a fire under my ass to finish this project and motivated me to do just that. Brandon Lorenz's strategic guidance and just really smart ideas have helped shape and give meaning to our work as an organization and to the words found within these pages. I am so blessed to work with so many creative and strategic people, including Tallman Trask, Clayton Spinney, Lance Orchid, Daniel Forkkio, Po Murray, Michelle Ringuette, Shira Goodwin, and Michael Fleming.

While writing this book, I was motivated and inspired by so many brilliant advocates and thinkers who have been working to build a future with fewer guns every single day, relentlessly, for years. Chief among them are Nina Vinik, Arkadi Gerney, Tim Daly, and Mark Glaze. These four brought me into this movement and helped me find my place within it. I will forever be grateful for their guidance and support. More broadly, I have to mention the amazing Sarah and Abby Clements, Stasha Rhodes, Mark Jones, Alicia Samuels, Amber Goodwin, Christian Heyne, Lori Haas, Josh Horwitz, Adam Skaggs, Josh Sugarmann, and so many others.

Throughout this journey, I've also relied on several friends who have been kind enough to look at different portions of this work and provide invaluable feedback. Josh Rovenger printed out the entire manuscript and read it while flying to his bachelor party! He's the reason why the introduction explains why I don't believe all firearms should be banned. Josh Lederman read a version on his computer, but offered no less valuable suggestions about chapter framing, order, and how best to pull the reader in. These two were the first "outsiders" to read the book in full, and their positive feedback gave me the confidence I needed to drive this project toward the finish line. I'm also forever indebted to Clara Salzberg, Matt Ingram, Ed Chung, Navin Nayak, Laura Merner, Jeff Krehely, Kerry Eleveld, Evan Wolfson, Michael Waldman, Michelangelo Signorile, and Errick McAdams, for their great encouragement and help with various parts of the book-writing process.

That process would never have been possible without my amazing literary agent, Anna Sproul-Latimer of Ross Yoon, who guided me through everything from A to Z and always had my back, and also Howard Yoon, who sharpened my book proposal with his keen insights. Julie Enszer, my editor at The New Press, put up with me and challenged me, and made this work so much better. Amanda Palleschi is the reason I was able to finish this book on any kind of reasonable timetable and insert the right level of detail, fact, and personal anecdote. A big thank-you to you, Amanda.

Working on a book is an incredibly time-consuming project that pushes everything else out of your life and forces those close to you to bear your burdens and responsibilities. This is something I may not have always recognized while going through this process, but I am very clear-eyed about this reality as I write these words now. I would not have been able to work through this project had it not been for the support and understanding of Brian Volsky. I certainly would not have been able to complete it without the love, tenderness, and sacrifices of Pete Dohan, who makes it possible for me to continue doing this work every single day. And finally, I want to thank my parents for instilling within me the drive, determination, and perseverance that pushed me to take on and complete this project.

APPENDIX: HOW TO TALK TO GUN PEOPLE AND WIN

If you take away one lesson from reading this book, let it be that in the long run, the best way to win an argument is to be armed with facts, not guns. Here is your guide for how to push back against the most common characters and arguments you are sure to encounter as you work to build a future with fewer guns.

The Derailer: This is the guy who stares at you calmly as you explain that allowing just anyone to waltz into a gun show and purchase a semiautomatic assault weapon has resulted in the deaths of thousands of people. He replies, "Well, it's not the guns that kill people; it's the people that kill people." You focus your eyes on his forehead to prevent them from rolling back into yours, then calmly launch into the Derailer pushback:

You know what, you're right. Guns themselves don't actually kill thirty thousand Americans each year—but they do make it really easy. And as long as you're pointing out that it's *people* who are doing all the killing, then let's actually restrict the kind of *people* who can get guns. After all, states with higher levels of gun ownership have gun murder rates up to 114 percent higher than states with low levels of gun ownership,[1] and a review of thirty years of crime data calculated that "for each percentage point increase in gun ownership, the firearm homicide rate increased by 0.9 percent."[2]

We already have all kinds of precedent for severely restricting access to inanimate objects that are dangerous or could become dangerous. Take cars, for example. If I were to say to you, "People shouldn't have to pass a test and get a license to legally drive a car; all we need to do is punish dangerous and reckless car owners," you'd probably think I was crazy. Nobody would seriously argue that we should allow people who don't know how to operate a motor vehicle to get on a highway and drive 75—okay, 80—miles an hour and *only* punish them if they hit another car and hurt somebody. We as a society have decided that we should protect our communities from people who don't know how to drive because they put us all at risk. Why not apply the same logic to supersonic-projectile launching devices? Fun fact: automobiles kill approximately thirty thousand people per year, about the same number who die from guns.[3]

The Doc: This is anyone without a medical degree who, upon engaging in a conversation about gun safety, suddenly grows concerned about the state of our mental health system and its inadequacy for treating people who are mentally unstable—thus leading them to get guns and commit crimes.

Response: Mental illness occurs in all countries, but the United States—with gun regulation loopholes big enough to drive a tank through—has three times the homicide rate of Canada and more than ten times that of Germany.[4] Moreover, a psychiatric diagnosis can predict gun violence, but other factors, like a history of violence and substance abuse—and access to guns—are far better indicators of future gun crimes.[5] Oh, and by the way, statistically speaking, mentally ill people commit only a tiny percentage of violent crime— an estimated 5 percent—and are actually far more likely to be the victims of violence. They are five times more likely to die by homicide than the general population and twice as likely to die by suicide.[6]

The Censor: "Back in my day, you didn't have the kind of gratuitous violence you kids are watching today. From movies to TV to video games: it's all stick 'em up and *bang bang bang*. No wonder many young men shoot up schools or movie theaters. They're just reenacting what they see in the media!"

Response: This argument is as old as media itself. Back in the 1920s, America's morality crusaders were very concerned that movies with sound—talkies!—were contributing to the delinquency of youth. In the early 1950s, the media's focus on teenagers and their bad habits similarly set off all sorts of alarm bells for reformists. Ultimately, the impact of media on people—you know, very complex human beings—is almost impossible to measure. How can you untangle the complex web that shapes and influences behavior—everything from mental health to parenting to socioeconomic status to friendships? To pull out violent movies or video games and argue that they're a primary cause of aggression or criminal activity is to ignore the many factors that can influence a person's decisions and actions. And of course the rest of the world watches the very same movies we do—yet has dramatically fewer gun deaths. In fact, a *Washington Post* analysis compared video game expenditures and violent crime rates in ten advanced industrial nations and found no relationship between increased video game playing and increased real-world killing.[7]

The Inanimate Objector: "Well, scissors and knives kill people too. Are you going to require people to apply for steak dinner licenses?"

Response: Okay, when was the last time you heard of a drive-by knifing or people dying en masse at Ruth's Chris? More than 75 percent of mass murderers kill with guns because they know (as do you) that guns are more lethal than other weapons—and provide killers with a more impersonal, antiseptic way of taking human life. A study that compared fatal and nonfatal gun and knife assaults in Chicago over a period of three years found that "gun attacks were about five times as likely to kill as knife attacks," and domestic assaults that involve firearms are three times more likely to result in death than those committed with knives.[8]

Uncle Tea Party: Perhaps you've met this guy across your Thanksgiving dinner table. "It's a slippery slope to government tyranny," your uncle says between his second and third helping of green bean casserole. You look down at his plate and then back at him, thinking that the way things are going, it's a slippery slope from Thanksgiving dinner to you punching him unconscious.

Response: Yes, everything can be a slippery slope. Yet we human beings have somehow managed to discern rational restrictions from extreme prohibitions: setting speed limits without completely outlawing driving, limiting how much cough syrup you can buy without pulling it off the shelves, and yes, even when it comes to guns, we've passed some sensible regulations without completely eliminating firearms. For instance, felons have been prohibited from owning guns since 1968, but you, dear Uncle Tea Party, are still allowed to own those eight rifles in your bedroom.

The Constitution-splainer: You know the type: MAKE AMERICA GREAT AGAIN hat, Confederate flag bumper sticker, American flag T-shirt. As soon as you say anything at all about guns, he flips open to the Second Amendment and recites it from memory. "A well regulated Militia, being necessary to the security of a free State, the right of the people to keep and bear Arms, shall not be infringed." He points to the text emphatically and demands, "Show me where it says you can prohibit me from buying guns!"

Response: Well, it's not in the actual text, but then again, none of the restrictions on our constitutional rights are. The First Amendment protects your freedom of speech, but as you probably know, it doesn't permit you to yell "Fire!" in a crowded theater or spread slander. Many of our individual rights stop where someone else's begin, and as Mr. Constitutional Originalist himself, Justice Antonin Scalia, pointed out in the 2008 Supreme Court case that recognized an individual's right to possess a firearm within the home, the rights spelled out in the Second Amendment can and should be limited. "Nothing in our opinion should be taken to cast doubt on longstanding prohibitions on the possession of firearms by felons and the mentally ill, or laws forbidding the carrying of firearms in sensitive places such as schools and government buildings, or laws imposing conditions and qualifications on the commercial sale of arms," he wrote, adding that the Court's decision supports the "historical tradition of prohibiting the carrying of 'dangerous and unusual weapons.'"

In fact, since we're on the topic, it's worth pointing out that during the constitutional period, major American cities like New York and Boston actually prohibited the firing of guns within city limits. Rhode Island conducted a house-by-house census of gun owners. Maryland prevented Catholics from owning firearms. Even the so-called Wild West had strict gun laws, despite the way it's often portrayed in popular movies and culture. Gun restrictions have been a part of our country for centuries and are as American as the Constitution itself.

The Existing Law Lover: This is the guy who—despite his great mistrust of the government—insists that rather than pass new laws, we must simply enforce the laws already on the books.

Response: The problem is that the existing laws suck—and are failing to keep guns out of the hands of killers and criminals. An estimated 40 percent of all gun sales go through private sellers who don't even have to run the three-minute background check required of licensed federal dealers.[9] That means we don't know who's buying what kind of guns or how many. One investigation discovered that 62 percent of online gun sellers were perfectly willing to sell to buyers who *admitted* that they were forbidden from buying a weapon from a licensed dealer. Bottom line: approximately 75 percent of the weapons used in mass shootings between 1982 and 2012 were purchased legally,[10] so there is clearly something inadequate about our current gun laws.

Oh, and by the way, it's always *so* rich to hear the NRA preach about enforcing existing gun laws. For decades the gun lobby has dedicated itself to weakening gun regulations and undermining enforcement. A short (and very incomplete) summary:

1. The NRA worked to defeat the current background check system legislatively and funded legal challenges once the Brady Bill became law, asking the Supreme Court to invalidate the entire statute, yet hypocritically it regularly criticizes Democratic administrations for failing to prosecute individuals who falsely claim on their background check form that they are not felons or otherwise prohibited from buying a gun.

2. The NRA successfully weakened the government's ability to prosecute gun dealers for failing to keep records of their gun sales, which is the only way for officials to trace guns involved in crimes.

3. The NRA undermined the government's ability to enforce the record-keeping requirements by limiting inspections to a single unannounced inspection every twelve months.

4. The NRA uses its influence over the appropriations process to push Republicans to underfund federal inspections, thus ensuring that most licensed dealers are inspected "infrequently or not at all."

5. The NRA secured a provision that prevents the government from establishing a centralized computer database of digital records that would allow it to easily trace the serial number of a gun used in a crime in order to help identify the criminal who used it.

The Stockpiler: Because I write and tweet and talk about guns, a lot of the people I meet offer to show me their guns. They're very proud to take me down to their dimly lit basement, unlock their large storage case, and expose fourteen semiautomatic weapons and sixty-two handguns. Yeehaw!

Response: My reaction is always the same. I'm impressed as they tell me the story behind each weapon. I appreciate how it just sings like a bird in their hands. But I can't help but think that a gun—never mind this many guns—is statistically four times more likely to be involved in an accidental shooting than to be used to injure or kill someone in self-defense.[11] Kids are particularly vulnerable, as one experiment found that a full third of eight- to twelve-year-old boys who come across a handgun actually pull the trigger—despite being counseled about how to behave safely around guns.[12] Households that keep firearms also have a fivefold increase in the risk of suicide—and when a gun is used, the fatality rate is 80 percent.[13]

The *Law & Order* Fan: In my experience, this is the elderly woman who watches *Law & Order* or *Criminal Minds* on repeat. She may have seen that episode already, but if it's on and you're there, she'll watch it with you! Should the subject of guns come up, she'll tell you, "Darlin', I've lived me some life, and I can tell you that if you start outlawing guns, the only people who'll have guns are the outlaws!"

Response: Actually, existing gun laws are already disarming outlaws. For instance, the National Firearms Act of 1934 effectively banned machine guns from circulation by taxing them. You don't hear about gangs roaming around with tommy guns precisely because gun restrictions work. And they do so in a targeted way. Just as the 1934 law severely restricted the availability of machine guns without wiping out all weapons, the 1993 background check law has stopped more than 2 million gun transactions—preventing outlaws from buying guns while preserving the rights of responsible gun owners to buy firearms. Some determined criminals will naturally try to skirt the law, but many will be deterred by it. For instance, one survey that asked criminals why they didn't carry a weapon in the commission of their crimes found that 79 percent cited "get a stiffer sentence" and 59 percent said it was because it was "against the law."[14] Another showed that individuals who were denied purchases of handguns because of prior felony conviction "were less likely to commit subsequent crimes than those who had been arrested but not convicted and thus were able to obtain handguns. Denial of a handgun purchase is associated with a reduction in risk for later criminal activity of approximately 20–30 percent."[15] Ultimately, the ability of criminals to skirt the law isn't a reason not to pass any laws at all. It's a reason to tighten them. This is true for laws against theft and murder and, of course, guns.

The Liam Neeson Character in *Taken***:** This guy fancies himself a Ninja avenger, a steel-jawed Man in Black wearing opaque shades. He keeps buying new guns to protect his family from intruders in the home or sex-slave abductors at the movie theater. He wears his cold heart on his sleeve: if other people know you love to shoot things, they'll be a lot less likely to mess with you, right?

Response: Sometimes the threat is real, and in some places it's continual. If you're strolling through downtown Baltimore or Kabul, carrying a gun for self-protection is reasonable. Unfortunately, regular people don't have the kind of specialized continuous training that Sam, police officers, and other law enforcement professionals undergo, training that shortens reaction time and builds muscle memory one can rely on in a crisis. Thus they often do more harm than good against an armed criminal, becoming easy targets for the killer or hitting innocent people with their bullets. That's why, from

2000 to 2013, twenty-one active shooters were stopped by unarmed civilians while just one was stopped by a civilian with a firearm.[16] Of course, it's not really your fault. Your body undermines your ability to react. As one ABC News simulation of gun owners forced to react to an armed assailant showed, "Under extreme stress, your blood is actually pulled from your skin toward your muscles in case you need to flee, your heart is pumping three or four times the normal rate, your hands have less blood, they're less dexterous, your reaction [is] delayed."[17] A study of seventy-seven volunteers who participated in three different scenarios—a carjacking, an armed robbery in a convenience store, and a larceny—found that those who had no specialized training performed poorly. "They didn't take cover. They didn't attempt to issue commands to their assailants. Their trigger fingers were either too itchy—they shot innocent bystanders or unarmed people, or not itchy enough—they didn't shoot armed assailants until they were already being shot at," the *Washington Post* reported.[18] The risk of keeping a firearm actually outweighs its benefits, as the probability of shootings or suicide increases greatly when you introduce more guns into your home or community. Gun ownership doesn't even deter burglars; in fact, one study found that a 10 percent increase in gun ownership increased burglary rates by 3 to 7 percent. The researchers assumed that the burglars specifically targeted gun-owning households to steal their guns and sell them.[19]

Ultimately, the truth of the matter is that Americans are far more likely to die in a homicide or suicide than commit an act of bravery and protect their families. In 2012, there were 258 justifiable killings, defined by the FBI as "the killing of a felon, during the commission of a felony, by a private citizen." Compare that to the 20,666 suicides by gun, and 8,855 criminal gun homicides. For every justifiable gun homicide in 2012, America experienced 34 criminal gun homicides, 78 gun suicides, and 2 accidental gun deaths.[20] That's part of the reason why the sixteen states with the highest rate of gun ownership have "more than four times as many gun suicides as the states with low gun ownership," and states with the highest gun death rates overall typically have weak gun laws.[21]

NOTES

Preface: Shooting Guns in the Desert Can Surprise You

1. John Gramlich, "5 Facts About Crime in the U.S.," Pew Research Center, January 30, 2018, http://www.pewresearch.org/fact-tank/2018/01/30/5-facts-about-crime-in-the-u-s.

Introduction: Why You Should Give Up Your Guns

1. Antonis Katsiyannis, Denise K. Whitford, and Robin Parks Ennis, "Historical Examination of United States Intentional Mass School Shootings in the 20th and 21st Centuries: Implications for Students, Schools, and Society," *Journal of Child and Family Studies*, April 2018, press release at *ScienceDaily*, www.sciencedaily.com/releases/2018/04/180419131025.htm.

It's Far Too Easy to Buy a Gun

1. "Universal Background Checks," Giffords Law Center to Prevent Gun Violence, http://lawcenter.giffords.org/gun-laws/policy-areas/background-checks/universal-background-checks.

Guns Kill Young People

1. Center for American Progress analysis of data from "Fatal Injury Reports, National, Regional and State, 1981–2016," WISQARS, Centers for Disease Control and Prevention, https://webappa.cdc.gov/sasweb/ncipc/mortrate.html.

2. David Hogg and Lauren Hogg, *#NeverAgain: A New Generation Draws the Line* (New York: Random House, 2018), Kindle ed., 10.

3. Nikki Graf, "A Majority of U.S. Teens Fear a Shooting Could Happen at Their School, and Most Parents Share Their Concern," Pew Research Center, April 18, 2018, www.pewresearch.org/fact-tank/2018/04/18/a-majority-of-u-s-teens-fear-a-shooting-could-happen-at-their-school-and-most-parents-share-their-concern; John Woodrow Cox et al., "More Than 215,000 Students Have Experienced Gun Violence at School Since Columbine," *Washington Post*, August 23, 2018.

4. Alexia Fernández Campbell, "After Parkland, a Push for More School Shooting Drills," *Vox*, March 14, 2018, www.vox.com/policy-and-politics/2018/2/16/17016382/school-shooting-drills-training.

5. Fernández Campbell, "After Parkland."

6. Lauren Rygg, "School Shooting Simulations: At What Point Does Preparation Become More Harmful Than Helpful?" *Children's Legal Rights Journal* 35, no. 3 (January 1, 2015), https://lawecommons.luc.edu/cgi/viewcontent.cgi?article=1106&context=clrj.

7. Rebecca Onion, "The Teacher Would Suddenly Yell 'Drop!'" *Slate*, March 13, 2018, https://slate.com/human-interest/2018/03/are-duck-and-cover-school-drills-from-the-nuclear-era-a-useful-parallel-to-active-shooter-drills.html.

Guns Kill People of Color

1. "Past Summary Ledgers," *Gun Violence Archive*, August 27, 2018, www.gunviolencearchive.org/past-tolls.

2. Anita Knopov, Molly Pahn, and Michael Siegel, "Gun Violence in the US Kills More Black People and Urban Dwellers," Boston University School of Public Health, https://www.bu.edu/sph/2017/11/15/gun-violence-in-the-us-kills-more-black-people-and-urban-dwellers.

3. David Hemenway and Elizabeth G. Richardson, "Homicide, Suicide, and Unintentional Firearm Fatality: Comparing the United States with Other High-Income Countries," *Journal of Trauma* 70, no. 1 (January 2011): 238–42.

4. Giffords, "Urban Gun Violence," https://giffords.org/issue/urban-gun-violence.

5. Everytown for Gun Safety, "Strategies for Reducing Gun Violence in American Cities," https://everytownresearch.org/reports/strategies-for-reducing-gun-violence-in-american-cities.

6. Mary Patillo et al., "Crime in Chicago: What Does the Research Tell Us?" Institute for Policy Research, Northwestern University, March 9, 2018, https://www.ipr.northwestern.edu/about/news/2018/crime-in-chicago-research.html.

7. Patillo, "Crime in Chicago."

8. Center for American Progress analysis of John Muyskens, "Fatal

Force," *Washington Post*, https://www.washingtonpost.com/graphics/2018/national/police-shootings-2018.

9. DeJuan Patterson, "How My Run-in with Gun Violence Inspired Me to Make an Impact in My Community," *Elite Daily*, September 20, 2016, https://www.elitedaily.com/news/politics/dejuan-patterson-shot-head-community/1617698.

10. Molly Bangs and Maya T. Miller, "Gun Violence Coverage, Consumption Paint False Reality," Century Foundation, August 1, 2016, https://tcf.org/content/commentary/gun-violence-coverage-consumption-paint-false-reality.

Guns Kill Women and Children

1. Katie McDonough, "'Where There Are More Guns, More Women Die': A Harvard Public Health Expert Breaks Down the Data on Firearms and Women's Safety," *Salon*, February 24, 2015.

2. Center for American Progress analysis of Supplemental Homicide Data, Federal Bureau of Investigation, U.S. Department of Justice, 2006–2015. "Intimate partner" includes boyfriends, girlfriends, husbands, wives, ex-wives, ex-husbands, common-law wives, and common-law husbands. The state of Florida does not report information to the FBI and therefore is not included in this analysis.

3. Winnie Stachelberg et al., "Preventing Domestic Abusers and Stalkers from Accessing Guns" (Washington: Center for American Progress, 2013), http://americanprogress.org/issues/civil-liberties/report/2013/05/09/60705/preventing-domestic-abusers-and-stalkers-from-accessing-guns.

4. Everytown for Gun Safety, "Guns and Domestic Violence," April 4, 2018, https://everytownresearch.org/guns-domestic-violence.

5. Everytown for Gun Safety, "Guns and Domestic Violence."

6. Evan DeFilippis and Devin Hughes, "Gun-Rights Advocates Claim Owning a Gun Makes a Woman Safer: The Research Says They're Wrong," *The Trace*, May 2, 2016, https://www.thetrace.org/2016/05/gun-ownership-makes-women-safer-debunked.

7. "Data Collection: National Crime Victimization Survey," Bureau of Justice Statistics, http://www.bjs.gov/index.cfm?ty=dcdetail&iid=245; Emily DePrang, "The Truth About Women and Guns," *Marie Claire*, February 11, 2016; and Evan DeFilippis, "Having a Gun in the House Doesn't Make a Woman Safer," *The Atlantic*, February 25, 2014.

8. Katherine A. Fowler et al., "Childhood Firearm Injuries in the United States," *Pediatrics* 140, no. 1 (June 2017).

9. Fowler, "Childhood Firearm Injuries."

We Are Killing Ourselves with Guns

1. Brady Center to Prevent Gun Violence, "Americans in Crisis: Access to Guns Increases Deaths by Suicide," September 2017, https://www.bradycampaign.org/sites/default/files/AmericansInCrisis-GunsAndSuicide_09-2017.pdf.

2. Center for American Progress analysis of Centers for Disease Control and Prevention, "Injury Prevention & Control: Data & Statistics (WISQARS): Fatal Injury Data." For both African Americans and white people, we selected non-Hispanic. The rate of gun homicides from 2007 to 2016 for young African Americans was 40.79 per every 100,000 people while the rate of white young people was 2.29.

3. "Firearm Access Is a Risk Factor for Suicide," Harvard School of Public Health, https://www.hsph.harvard.edu/means-matter/means-matter/risk.

4. Deborah M. Stone et al., "Vital Signs: Trends in State Suicide Rates—United States, 1999–2016, and Circumstances Contributing to Suicide—27 States, 2015," *Morbidity and Mortality Weekly Report*, Centers for Disease Control and Prevention, June 07, 2018, https://www.cdc.gov/mmwr/volumes/67/wr/mm6722a1.htm.

5. Jen Christensen, "LGBQ Teens Face Serious Suicide Risk, Research Finds," CNN, December 19, 2017, https://www.cnn.com/2017/12/19/health/lgbq-teens-suicide-risk-study/index.html.

6. Ann P. Haas, Philip L. Rodgers, and Jody L. Herman, "Suicide Attempts Among Transgender and Gender Non-conforming Adults: Findings of the National Transgender Discrimination Survey," January 2014, Williams Institute, UCLA School of Law, https://williamsinstitute.law.ucla.edu/wp-content/uploads/AFSP-Williams-Suicide-Report-Final.pdf.

How I Became a Fewer-Guns Activist

1. Ashby Jones and Dan Frosch, "Rifles Used in San Bernardino Shooting Illegal Under State Law," *Wall Street Journal*, December 4, 2015.

2. Tom Kertscher, "Do 90% of Americans Support Background Checks for All Gun Sales?" *Politifact*, October 3, 2017, https://www.politifact.com/wisconsin/statements/2017/oct/03/chris-abele/do-90-americans-support-background-checks-all-gun-.

3. Igor Volsky, Archived "Thoughts and Prayers" Tweets, December 2, 2015, http://observer.com/2015/12/journalist-exposes-lawmakers-who-received-nra-donations-becomes-twitter-sensation.

4. John Bonazzo, "Journalist Exposes Lawmakers Who Received NRA Donations, Becomes Twitter Sensation," December 3, 2015, http://observer.com/2015/12/journalist-exposes-lawmakers-who-received-nra-donations-becomes-twitter-sensation.

The Founding Fathers Wanted a Country with Fewer Guns

1. Ronald Reagan, "Remarks at the Annual Members Banquet of the National Rifle Association in Phoenix, Arizona," May 6, 1983, American Presidency Project, http://www.presidency.ucsb.edu/ws/?pid=41289.

2. "Remarks by President Trump at the National Rifle Association Leadership Forum," April 28, 2017, https://www.whitehouse.gov/briefings-statements/remarks-president-trump-national-rifle-association-leadership-forum.

3. Saul Cornell, *A Well-Regulated Militia: The Founding Fathers and the Origins of Gun Control in America* (New York: Oxford University Press, 2008), Kindle ed., 2.

4. Cornell, *Well-Regulated Militia*, 27.

5. *District of Columbia et al. v. Dick Anthony Heller,* 554 U.S. 570 (2008), brief of amici curiae, http://www.scotusblog.com/wp-content/uploads/2008/01/07-290_amicus_historians.pdf.

6. Cornell, *Well-Regulated Militia*, 43.

7. Michael Waldman, *The Second Amendment: A Biography* (New York: Simon & Schuster, 2014), Kindle ed., 29.

8. *DC v. Heller,* 554 U.S. 570 (2008), brief of amici curiae.

9. Waldman, *Second Amendment.*

10. Roxanne Dunbar-Ortiz, *Loaded: A Disarming History of the Second Amendment* (San Francisco: City Lights, 2018), Kindle ed., 35, quoting Gaillard Hunt, ed., *The Writings of James Madison*, vol. 5, p. 319.

11. Waldman, *Second Amendment*, 55–56.

12. Waldman, *Second Amendment*, 55–56.

13. *DC v. Heller,* 554 U.S. 570 (2008), brief of amici curiae.

The NRA: Birth of a Lobby

1. Josh Sugarmann, *NRA: Money, Firepower, Fear* (Washington, DC: Violence Policy Center, rev. ed. 2010), 27.

2. U.S. House of Representatives, Committee on Ways and Means, 73rd Congress, 2nd Session, Hearings on H.R. 9066, National Firearms Act, April 16, 18 and May 14–16, 1934.

3. "Disarmament by Subterfuge," *American Rifleman*, May 1934.

4. Robert Sherrill, *The Saturday Night Special* (New York: Charterhouse, 1973).

5. Frances Stead Sellers, "How the Assassinations of 1968 Led the NRA to Become the Lobbying Force It Is Today," *Washington Post*, May 29, 2018.

6. Sugarmann, *NRA*, 48.

7. Laura Smith, "The Man Responsible for the Modern NRA Killed a Hispanic Teenager, Before Becoming a Border Agent," *Timeline*, July 6, 2017, https://timeline.com/harlon-carter-nra-murder-2f8227f2434f.

8. Erin Blakemore, "The Largest Mass Deportation in American History," History.com, March 23, 2018, https://www.history.com/news /operation-wetback-eisenhower-1954-deportation.

9. Smith, "The Man Responsible for the Modern NRA."

10. Robert J. Spitzer, *The Politics of Gun Control*, 7th ed. (Philadelphia: Taylor & Francis, 2017), Kindle ed.

How the NRA Weaponized the Second Amendment

1. Michael Waldman, *The Second Amendment: A Biography* (New York: Simon & Schuster, 2014), Kindle ed., 98.

2. Waldman, *Second Amendment*, 101.

3. "From Thomas Jefferson to George Washington, 19 June 1796," Founders Online, National Archives and Records Administration, https://founders.archives.gov/documents/Jefferson/01-29-02-0091.

4. Waldman, *Second Amendment*, 102.

5. David Cole, *Engines of Liberty: The Power of Citizen Activists to Make Constitutional Law* (New York: Basic Books, 2016), Kindle ed., 123.

6. "Post-*Heller* Litigation Summary," Law Center to Prevent Gun Violence, April 2017, http://lawcenter.giffords.org/wp-content/uploads/2017 /04/Post-Heller-Litigation-Summary-2017-April.pdf.

Why the NRA Is Successful

1. Nicole DuPuis et al., "City Rights in an Era of Preemption: A State-by-State Analysis," Center for City Solutions, National League of Cities, April 2, 2018, https://www.nlc.org/resource/city-rights-in-an-era -of-preemption-a-state-by-state-analysis.

2. Bruce Drake, "5 Facts About the NRA and Guns in America," Pew Research Center, April 24, 2014, http://www.pewresearch.org/fact-tank /2014/04/24/5-facts-about-the-nra-and-guns-in-america.

3. Chris W. Cox, "Mission Focused: The NRA's Legislative Agenda Looks to a Freer, Safer America," NRA-ILA, August 1, 2017, https:// www.nraila.org/articles/20170801/mission-focused-the-nra-s-legislative -agenda-looks-to-a-freer-safer-america.

4. Cox, "Mission Focused."

How the NRA Channels Hatred into Political Success

1. "Wayne LaPierre, on the Ropes," *New York Times*, May 20, 1995.

2. Charlton Heston, "Address to the Free Congress Foundation's 20th Anniversary Gala," Montgomery Citizens for a Safer America, December 20, 1997, https://www.mcsm.org/heston2.html; for the excerpt, quoted from a slightly longer version of December 7, see NRA on the Record, http://nraontherecord.org/charlton-heston; and for a thorough analysis, see Eliana Rae Eitches, "The National Rifle Association and the White Male Identity," Columbia University, December 21, 2012, https://academiccommons.columbia.edu/download/fedora_content /download/ac:156096/content/NRAotherizationRATD.pdf.

3. Violence Policy Center, "Lessons Unlearned: The Gun Lobby and the Siren Song of Anti-Government Rhetoric," April 2010, http://www .vpc.org/studies/lessonsunlearned.pdf.

4. "Dana Loesch Has a New Show Coming to NRATV," YouTube, February 14, 2018, https://www.youtube.com/watch?v=6dcFEAZQql8.

The New Second Amendment Compact

1. "Homicide," Injury Control Research Center, Harvard School of Public Health, June 30, 2016, https://www.hsph.harvard.edu/hicrc /firearms-research/guns-and-death.

2. Michael Siegel, Craig S. Ross, and Charles King III, "The Relationship Between Gun Ownership and Firearm Homicide Rates in the United States, 1981–2010," *American Journal of Public Health* 103, no. 11 (November 2013): 2098–2105, https://ajph.aphapublications.org/doi/abs/10.2105 /AJPH.2013.301409; and D. Mark Anderson, Daniel I. Rees, and Joseph J. Sabia, "Medical Marijuana Laws and Suicides by Gender and Age," *American Journal of Public Health* 104, no 12 (December 2014): 2369–76, https://ajph.aphapublications.org/doi/10.2105/AJPH.2013.301612.

3. "FBI Releases Study on Active Shooter Incidents," Federal Bureau of Investigation, September 24, 2014, https://www.fbi.gov/news/stories /fbi-releases-study-on-active-shooter-incidents.

4. "Mass Shootings in the United States: 2009–2016," Everytown Research.org, April 11, 2017, https://everytownresearch.org/reports/mass -shootings-analysis.

End Gun Manufacturer Immunity

1. Daniel W. Webster et al., "Effects of Undercover Police Stings of Gun Dealers on the Supply of New Guns to Criminals," *Injury Prevention* 12, no. 4 (August 2006): 225–30, https://www.ncbi.nlm.nih.gov/pmc /articles/PMC2586780.

2. Eli Rosenberg and Kristin Hussey, "Judge Dismisses Suit Against Gun Maker by Newtown Victims' Families," *New York Times*, December 21, 2017.

Increase Oversight and Regulation of Gun Manufacturers

1. "Design Safety Standards," Giffords Law Center to Prevent Gun Violence, http://lawcenter.giffords.org/gun-laws/policy-areas/child-consumer -safety/design-safety-standards.
2. "Design Safety Standards."

Regulate All Gun Dealers

1. Everytown for Gun Safety, "Strategies for Reducing Gun Violence in American Cities," n. 18, https://everytownresearch.org/reports/strategies -for-reducing-gun-violence-in-american-cities/#foot_note_anchor_18.
2. "Strategies for Reducing Gun Violence."

Reduce the Number of Guns in the United States

1. Mayors Against Illegal Guns, "Analysis of Recent Mass Shootings," January 2013, http://libcloud.s3.amazonaws.com/9/56/4/1242/1/analysis -of-recent-mass-shootings.pdf, 1.
2. House of Representatives, 115th Congress, 2017–18 Session, Hearings on H.R. 5490, Handgun Purchaser Licensing Act, https://www .congress.gov/bill/115th-congress/house-bill/5490/text.

A License to Kill

1. Sarah Richards, "Why Background Checks for Gun Purchases Have Gun-Owner Support," *Johns Hopkins Magazine*, September 11, 2015, http: //hub.jhu.edu/magazine/2015/fall/background-checks-guns.
2. Daniel W. Webster, Cassandra Kircher Crifasi, and Jon S. Vernick, "Effects of Missouri's Repeal of Its Handgun Purchaser Licensing Law on Homicides," Center for Gun Policy and Research, Bloomberg School of Public Health, Johns Hopkins University, December 17, 2013, https: //www.jhsph.edu/research/centers-and-institutes/johns-hopkins-center -for-gun-policy-and-research/_pdfs/effects-of-missouris-repeal-of-its -handgun-purchaser-licensing-law-on-homicides.pdf.
3. Center for Gun Policy and Research, "Permit-to-Purchase Licensing for Handguns," March 2015, Center for Gun Policy and Research, Bloomberg School of Public Health, Johns Hopkins University, https://www.jhsph.edu/research/centers-and-institutes/johns-hopkins

-center-for-gun-policy-and-research/publications/FactSheet_Permit toPurchaseLicensing.pdf.

4. Center for Gun Policy and Research, "Permit-to-Purchase Licensing for Handguns."

5. Giffords Law Center to Prevent Gun Violence, "Safe Storage," http://lawcenter.giffords.org/gun-laws/policy-areas/child-consumer -safety/safe-storage.

6. "Number of Mass Shootings in the United States Between 1982 and 2018, by Shooter's Gender," Statista, https://www.statista.com/statistics /476445/mass-shootings-in-the-us-by-shooter-s-gender.

7. Giffords Law Center, "Safe Storage."

8. Giffords Law Center, "Safe Storage."

9. Cassandra K. Crifasi et al., "Association Between Firearm Laws and Homicide in Urban Counties," *Journal of Urban Health* 95, no. 3 (June 2018): 383–90, https://link.springer.com/article/10.1007/s11524-018-0273-3.

Insure Your Piece

1. Peter Kochenburger, "Liability Insurance and Gun Violence," University of Connecticut Faculty Articles and Papers, 2014, https://opencommons .uconn.edu/cgi/viewcontent.cgi?article=1225&context=law_papers.

2. Michelle Singletary, "The Enormous Economic Cost of Gun Violence," *Washington Post*, February 22, 2018.

Unleash the Power of Science to Save Lives

1. "Removing Barriers and Reinvesting in Public Health Research on Gun Violence," Center for American Progress, https://www.americanprogress .org/issues/guns-crime/reports/2016/03/09/132894/removing-barriers -and-reinvesting-in-public-health-research-on-gun-violence.

2. Christine Jamieson, "Gun Violence Research: History of the Federal Funding Freeze," *Monitor on Psychology*, American Psychological Association, February 2013, http://www.apa.org/science/about/psa/2013/02/gun -violence.aspx.

3. Sam Roberts, "Jay Dickey, Arkansas Lawmaker Who Blocked Gun Research, Dies at 77," *New York Times*, April 24, 2017.

Reducing Gun Violence in Chicago

1. Shelby Bremer, "Most Guns in Chicago Crimes Come from out of State: Report," NBC 5 Chicago, October 31, 2017, https://www .nbcchicago.com/blogs/ward-room/chicago-gun-trace-report-2017 -454016983.html.

2. Everytown for Gun Safety, "Strategies for Reducing Gun Violence in American Cities," n. 18, https://everytownresearch.org/reports /strategies-for-reducing-gun-violence-in-american-cities/#foot _note_anchor_18.

How to Eliminate Mass Shootings

1. German Lopez, "The Research Is Clear: Gun Control Saves Lives," *Vox*, October 4, 2017, https://www.vox.com/policy-and-politics/2017/10 /4/16418754/gun-control-washington-post.

The Solutions in the Compact Have Worked in the Rest of the World

1. Zack Beauchamp, "America Doesn't Have More Crime than Other Rich Countries: It Just Has More Guns," *Vox*, February 15, 2018, https://www.vox.com/2015/8/27/9217163/america-guns-europe.

2. Everytown for Gun Safety, "Strategies for Reducing Gun Violence in American Cities," n. 18.

3. Aaron Karp, "Estimating Global Civilian-Held Firearms Numbers," Small Arms Survey, Briefing Paper, June 2018, http://www .smallarmssurvey.org/fileadmin/docs/T-Briefing-Papers/SAS-BP -Civilian-Firearms-Numbers.pdf.

4. Erin Grinshteyn et al., "Violent Death Rates: The US Compared with Other High-income OECD Countries," *American Journal of Medicine* 129, no. 3 (2010): 266–73, https://www.amjmed.com/action /showCitFormats?pii=S0002-9343(15)01030-X&doi=10.1016/j.amjmed .2015.10.025.

5. Michael Hiltzik, "After Its Own Mass Shootings, Germany Beefed Up Gun Control Laws: The Number of Shootings Dropped," *Los Angeles Times*, June 15, 2016.

6. David Hemenway, *Private Guns, Public Health* (Ann Arbor: University of Michigan Press, 2004), Kindle loc. 355–57.

Gun Owners Support a World with Fewer Guns

1. Maj Toure as told to Mike Spies, "Urban Gun Violence as Seen by a Black Second Amendment Activist," *The Trace*, August 19, 2016, https://www.thetrace.org/2016/08/black-guns-matter-urban-violence.

How You Can Build a Future with Fewer Guns

1. Aaron Blake, "Manchin-Toomey Gun Amendment Fails," *Washington Post*, April 17, 2013.

Learning from the Fight for Marriage Equality

1. "Evan Wolfson," Freedom to Marry, http://freedomtomarry.org/the
-team/entry/Evan-Wolfson.

A Strategy for Building a World with Fewer Guns

1. Arkadi Gerney and Chelsea Parsons, "License to Kill: How Lax Concealed Carry Laws Can Combine with Stand Your Ground Laws to Produce Deadly Results" (Washington, DC: Center for American Progress, September 2013), https://cdn.americanprogress.org/wp-content /uploads/2013/09/StandYrGround.pdf.

2. Bobby Allyn, "Some 3D Printing Companies Are Taking Action Against Gun Blueprints," NPR, August 14, 2018, https://www.npr.org /2018/08/14/638629404/some-3d-printing-companies-are-taking-action -against-gun-blueprints.

3. Mariella Moon, "Senators Want Google and Facebook to Block 3D-printed Gun Files," *Engadget*, August 17, 2018, https://www .engadget.com/2018/08/17/senators-urge-tech-giants-block-3d-printed -gun-files.

We Will Win

1. Harry Enten, "There's a Gun for Every American, but Less Than a Third Own Guns," CNN, February 15, 2018, https://www.cnn.com/2018 /02/15/politics/guns-dont-know-how-many-america/index.html.

2. Giffords, "Gun Safety Activism Spurred Action as 26 States Pass 55 Laws to Address Gun Violence Crisis," July 23, 2018, https://giffords.org /2018/07/midyear-trendwatch.

Appendix: How to Talk to Gun People and Win

1. Matthew Miller, David Hemenway, and Deborah Azrael, "State-Level Homicide Victimization Rates in the US in Relation to Survey Measures of Household Firearm Ownership, 2001–2003," *Social Science &*

Medicine 64, no. 3 (February 2007): 656–64, https://www.deepdyve.com/lp/elsevier/state-level-homicide-victimization-rates-in-the-us-in-relation-to-TNMKd0qUVn.

2. Michael Siegel, Craig S. Ross, and Charles King III, "The Relationship Between Gun Ownership and Firearm Homicide Rates in the United States, 1981–2010," *American Journal of Public Health* 103, no. 11 (November 2013): 2098–2105, https://ajph.aphapublications.org/doi/abs/10.2105/AJPH.2013.301409; and D. Mark Anderson, Daniel I. Rees, and Joseph J. Sabia, "Medical Marijuana Laws and Suicides by Gender and Age," *American Journal of Public Health* 104, no 12 (December 2014): 2369–76, https://ajph.aphapublications.org/doi/10.2105/AJPH.2013.301612.

3. Christopher Ingraham, "Guns Are Now Killing as Many People as Cars in the U.S.," *Washington Post*, December 17, 2015.

4. Kevin Quealy and Margot Sanger-Katz, "Comparing Gun Deaths by Country: The U.S. Is in a Different World," *New York Times*, June 21, 2018.

5. Jonathan M. Metzl and Kenneth T. MacLeish, "Mental Illness, Mass Shootings, and the Politics of American Firearms," *American Journal of Public Health* 105, no. 2 (February 2015): 240–49, doi:10.2105/ajph.2014.302242.

6. Jutta Lindert, "Violence Exposure and Mental Health States," *Violence and Mental Health: Its Manifold Faces*, ed. Jutta Lindert and Itzhak Levav (New York: Springer, 2015), ch. 3, pp. 47–69, doi:10.1007/978-94-017-8999-8_3.

7. Max Fisher, "Ten-Country Comparison Suggests There's Little or No Link Between Video Games and Gun Murders," *Washington Post*, December 17, 2012.

8. Dennis A. Henigan, *Guns Don't Kill People, People Kill People and Other Myths About Gun Control* (Boston: Beacon Press, 2016), 27.

9. Caroline Wolf Harlow, "Firearm Use by Offenders," Bureau of Justice Statistics, November 4, 2001, http://www.bjs.gov/index.cfm?ty=pbdetail&iid=940.

10. Mark Follman, Gavin Aronsen, and Deanna Pan, "A Guide to Mass Shootings in America," *Mother Jones*, June 28, 2018, http://www.motherjones.com/politics/2012/07/mass-shootings-map.

11. Henigan, *Guns Don't Kill People*, 18.

12. Geoffrey A. Jackman et al., "Seeing Is Believing: What Do Boys Do When They Find a Real Gun?" *Pediatrics* 107, no. 6 (June 2001): 1247–50, http://pediatrics.aappublications.org/content/107/6/1247.abstract.

13. Henigan, *Guns Don't Kill People*, 69.

14. Henigan, *Guns Don't Kill People*, 48.

15. Henigan, *Guns Don't Kill People*, 50.

16. Evan DeFilippis and Devin Hughes, "Gun-Rights Advocates Say Places That Ban Guns Attract Mass Shooters: The Data Says They're Wrong," *The Trace*, May 15, 2018, https://www.thetrace.org/2015/06/gun -rights-advocates-say-that-places-that-ban-guns-attract-mass-shooters -the-data-says-theyre-wrong.

17. "Proof That Concealed-Carry Permit Holders Live in a Dream World," Part 1, VPCvideos, YouTube, April 21, 2010, https://www .youtube.com/watch?v=8QjZY3WiO9s.

18. Christopher Ingraham, "Watch What Happens When Regular People Try to Use Handguns in Self-Defense," *Washington Post*, July 28, 2015.

19. Henigan, *Guns Don't Kill People*, 105.

20. Christopher Ingraham, "Guns in America: For Every Criminal Killed in Self-Defense, 34 Innocent People Die," *Washington Post*, June 19, 2015.

21. Philip J. Cook and Kristin A. Goss, *The Gun Debate: What Everyone Needs to Know* (New York: Oxford University Press, 2014), Kindle ed., 21.

INDEX

ABOUT THE AUTHOR

Igor Volsky is the co-founder and executive director of Guns Down America, an organization dedicated to building a future with fewer guns. Born in the former Soviet Union, Volsky immigrated to the United States with his family in 1993 and has been interested in politics and policy as early as he can remember. After spending years working for progressive change at the Center for American Progress, Volsky made international headlines in 2015 for shaming lawmakers who took money from the NRA and sent "thoughts and prayers" after mass shootings. *Guns Down* is Volsky's second book. A fixture on cable news and talk radio, he lives in Washington, DC.

PUBLISHING IN THE
PUBLIC INTEREST

Thank you for reading this book published by The New Press. The New Press is a nonprofit, public interest publisher. New Press books and authors play a crucial role in sparking conversations about the key political and social issues of our day.

We hope you enjoyed this book and that you will stay in touch with The New Press. Here are a few ways to stay up to date with our books, events, and the issues we cover:

- Sign up at www.thenewpress.com/subscribe to receive updates on New Press authors and issues and to be notified about local events.
- Like us on Facebook: www.faccbook.com/newpressbooks.
- Follow us on Twitter: www.twitter.com/thenewpress.

Please consider buying New Press books for yourself; for friends and family; or to donate to schools, libraries, community centers, prison libraries, and other organizations involved with the issues our authors write about.

The New Press is a 501(c)(3) nonprofit organization. You can also support our work with a tax-deductible gift by visiting www.thenewpress.com/donate.